# THE U.S. CONSTITUTION

Explained—Clause by Clause—
for Every American Today

# THE U.S. CONSTITUTION

Explained—Clause by Clause—
for Every American Today

Annotated by
*Ray Raphael*

Vintage Books
A Division of Penguin Random House LLC
New York

**FIRST VINTAGE BOOKS EDITION, OCTOBER 2017**

*Copyright © 2016, 2017 by Ray Raphael*

All rights reserved. Published in the United States by Vintage Books, a division of Penguin Random House LLC, New York, and distributed in Canada by Random House of Canada, a division of Penguin Random House Canada Limited, Toronto. Originally published in slightly different form as an original eShort by Vintage Books, a division of Penguin Random House LLC, New York, in 2016.

Vintage and colophon are registered trademarks of Penguin Random House LLC.

Library of Congress Cataloging-in-Publication Data
Names: Raphael, Ray, author.
Title: The U.S. Constitution : explained—clause by clause—for every American today / Ray Raphael.
Other titles: United States Constitution | U.S. Constitution
Description: First Vintage Books Edition. |
New York : Vintage, 2017.
Identifiers: LCCN 2017036856 (print) |
LCCN 2017037260 (ebook) | ISBN 9780525562542 (paperback) | ISBN 9780525562917 (ebook)
Subjects: LCSH: United States. Constitution. | Constitutional law—United States. | BISAC: LAW / Constitutional. | HISTORY / United States / Revolutionary Period (1775–1800).
Classification: LCC KF4550.R37 2017 (print) |
LCC KF4550 (ebook) | DDC 342.7302—dc23
LC record available at https://lccn.loc.gov/2017036856

**Vintage Books Trade Paperback ISBN: 978-0-525-56254-2
eBook ISBN: 978-0-525-56291-7**

*Book design by Steven Walker*

www.vintagebooks.com

Printed in the United States of America
10  9  8  7  6  5  4  3  2  1

# CONTENTS

# THE U.S. CONSTITUTION

Explained—Clause by Clause—
for Every American Today

## INTRODUCTION

In the United States, the Constitution—not
the president, nor any elected leader—reigns
supreme. Article VI declares succinctly: "This
Constitution, and the Laws of the United
States which shall be made in Pursuance
thereof, . . . shall be the supreme Law of the
Land." Americans for more than two centuries have treated the primacy of the Constitution as gospel, and that is no small part of
our endurance as a nation. "Regime change"
in the United States proceeds peacefully. One
president passes the torch to the next, even if
the two belong to opposing political parties.
Representatives and senators come and go,
but the Constitution provides the framework
under which they all must govern.

Yet the passage of time does present inter-
pretive problems. We have agreed to abide
by rules developed in a very different age. If
we are to understand the historical Constitution and allow it to guide us today, we need

to take account of the differences between then and now.

The framers' concerns were not identical to ours. The Constitution stipulates that Congress has the authority to "grant Letters of Marque and Reprisal" and "punish Piracies and Felonies committed on the high seas," but we worry more about terrorists on airplanes than pirates on the high seas. How can we balance airport security with privacy concerns? It would be odd to treat the framers as experts in such matters. We might look to basic principles that they espoused, but the devil is in the details and details are markedly absent.

Textual interpretation of the Constitution must account for the evolution of language. Article VI guarantees that the federal government will protect against "domestic Violence." Today the term refers to spousal abuse, but back then it meant civil unrest. Constitutionese is not our native tongue.

To grasp the context in which our Constitution was drafted, imagine that it is the spring of 1787. Under the Articles of Confederation, Congress depends on the states for funds, but from October 1786 through March 1787, the states have paid a grand total of $663 into the federal treasury. To use a modern idiom, the federal government has shrunk to the size where it can drown in a bathtub. Penniless and powerless, Congress cannot even muster a quorum.

The state of Massachusetts has asked Congress to suppress a rebellion ("domestic Violence") of indebted farmers who are closing the courts, but there is no federal army to speak of, only a few hundred soldiers stationed in western forts. Debtors are closing courts in South Carolina, Virginia, Maryland, and New Jersey as well. In Pennsylvania, farmers are preventing tax collectors from seizing their cattle. The Rhode Island legislature, under the sway of debtors, has just issued paper money. New York, North Carolina, and Georgia are now debating whether to follow Rhode Island's lead. All of this is destroying public credit. With the value of money plummeting, neither Congress nor the states can find willing lenders.

What is to be done? Obviously, the Articles of Confederation—the nation's existing constitution—need to be fixed. Twelve states (but not Rhode Island) send delegates to a convention in Philadelphia "for the sole and express purpose of revising the Articles of Confederation" to "render the federal constitution adequate to the exigencies of Government & the preservation of the Union." But will "revising" the Articles suffice? That document requires unanimous approval for any amendments, a hurdle that has proved impossible to clear. Two amendments granting Congress the power to lay imposts have already failed.

On the first day of deliberations, Virginia's Edmund Randolph and Pennsylvania's Gouverneur Morris move that instead of merely "correcting and enlarging" the Articles of Confederation, "a *national* government ought to be established consisting of a *supreme* legislative, executive & judiciary." (James Madison's meticulous notes on the convention emphasized the words "national" and "supreme.") Would delegates vote for it despite their instructions only to revise the Articles of Confederation?

They did, and that was a defining moment. The framers wanted to create from scratch an "energetic" government with sufficient "vigor" (among their favorite words) to prevent the United States from collapsing as a nation. A writer in *The Pennsylvania Gazette* put it this way: "The Year 1776 is celebrated for a revolution in favor of *Liberty*. The year 1787, it is expected, will be celebrated with equal joy, for a revolution in favor of *Government*."

What would that government look like?

The framers wanted it to be robust yet not tyrannical. To balance strength and restraint, they created three distinct branches that could constrain one another. "Separation of powers" and "checks and balances" are often said to limit federal power, but in fact, they serve the opposite purpose. By distributing authority to different components *within* the federal government, the framers gave that government *greater* powers than it dared grant to a single body. As protections grew, they could add more powers—that was the framers' basic strategy and crowning achievement.

The framers organized the Constitution around these centers of authority. Article I covers the legislative branch, Article II the executive branch, and Article III the judicial branch.

Article IV delineates the relationship among the states and between each state and the federal government.

Article V provides multiple methods for amending the Constitution. The fatal flaw of the Articles of Confederation was its inflexibility; requiring unanimity meant, in practice, that the Articles would never be amended. The framers knew their plan was not perfect and provided alternate routes, and a lower threshold, for amending it.

Article VI establishes the "Authority of the United States, . . . any Thing in the Constitution or Laws of any State to the Contrary notwithstanding."

Article VII stipulates the method of ratification. The plan the framers devised could not take effect unless the people approved it.

Ratification was by no means a foregone conclusion. The proposed Constitution transferred many powers formerly held by sovereign states to a new federal government. Only a few years past, Americans had rejected British rule, and many now feared that creating a powerful central government was not the best idea.

The framers' handiwork needed a persuasive introduction. Near the close of the convention, before releasing their proposal, delegates approved a preamble that explained what they were doing and why. That is where we start, at the beginning.

# Part One

# THE ORIGINAL CONSTITUTION

## PREAMBLE

**We the People of the United States, in Order to form a more perfect Union, establish Justice, insure domestic Tranquility, provide for the common defence, promote the general Welfare, and secure the Blessings of Liberty to ourselves and our Posterity, do ordain and establish this Constitution for the United States of America.**

*We the People of the United States . . . do ordain and establish this Constitution*: The next-to-last draft of the Constitution read: "We the people of the States of New Hampshire, Massachusetts, Rhode-Island and Providence Plantations . . ." and so on, listing the states north to south. But Rhode Island, which had refused to send delegates, might refuse to ratify, as might other states. If so, the Constitution would need to be amended immediately, deleting the missing state or states—a farcical reminder of the lack of unanimity. They had no choice but to jettison the state list. Besides, unlike the Articles of Confederation, which was a compact among states, the framers considered the Constitution a compact between the people and their government. For a nation based on popular sovereignty, *We the People* are the only ones entitled to *ordain and establish* a constitution.

*in Order to form a more perfect Union, establish Justice, insure domestic Tranquility, provide for the common defence, promote the general Welfare, and secure the Blessings of Liberty to ourselves and our Posterity:* In this sweeping enumeration of overarching goals, *general Welfare* and *Blessings of Liberty* stand next to each other without the slightest hint of conflict between them. Today, by contrast, they are often viewed as contradictory. *Liberty* connotes people doing as they please without interference or regulation, whereas *Welfare* denotes government handouts and *general Welfare* hints at socialism. Much of what the framers intended, hoped, or expected is lost in these distorted translations. The framers used *general Welfare* to signify the "common good" or "public good," terms they used frequently at the Constitutional Convention. *Liberty*, meanwhile, was public as well as private—to understand public liberty, think of the Revolutionary War and the Declaration of Independence.

In those times, government did not necessarily undercut liberty. A monarchical government might do so, an imperial government might do so, or a government that is too weak might do so, but a republican government, carefully conceived to promote the general welfare and rooted in the collective will of the people, could protect liberty by discreetly exerting authority. People were safest under a vigorous and effective government, imbued with sufficient powers to keep the ambitious few or the mindless many from trampling their rights.

The preamble, succinct yet sweeping, is civic poetry at its finest. However, it does not translate to constitutional law. Justice, defence, Welfare, Liberty—these are too general to provide the basis for judicial determinations.

## ARTICLE. I.

### SECTION. 1.

**All legislative Powers herein granted shall be vested in a Congress of the United States, which shall consist of a Senate and House of Representatives.**

In the beginning, there was Congress. Under the Articles of Confederation, "the United States in Congress assembled" was the only operative body binding the nation. Executive functions were handled by committees and boards; there were no federal judges because there were no federal laws. Congress determined policy, but it had no way of enforcing its will.

Although the new framework featured three distinct branches, Congress remained primary in two respects: it initiated legislation, and it represented the people—or at least one of the chambers did. What about the other? And why the need for two distinct chambers?

There were plenty of precedents. The House of Commons and the House of Lords in the British Parliament; the Assembly and Council in colonial governments; and the Assembly and Senate in state governments.

(Only Pennsylvania and Georgia were uni-
cameral, meaning one legislative chamber;
all other states were bicameral.) The "first
branch" or "lower house" (in the framers' parlance) was considered "democratic"
because it was supposed to represent the
people. Precisely *because* the lower house
represented the people's will, however,
the framers believed it was prone to wild
shifts and excessive actions. An upper house,
which the framers called the Senate, could
check such excesses. According to Virginia's
Edmund Randolph, "The democratic licen-
tiousness of the State Legislatures proved
the necessity of a firm Senate. The object
of this 2d. branch is to controul the democratic branch of the Natl. Legislature." James
Madison pronounced that the task of the
Senate was "to protect the people agst.
[against] the transient impressions into which
they themselves might be led." (Constitutional Convention quotes come from James
Madison's notes.) Sections 2 and 3, below,
reflect the distinct roles and constituencies of
the two houses.

## SECTION. 2.

**(1) The House of Representatives shall
be composed of Members chosen every**

second Year by the People of the several States, and the Electors in each State shall have the Qualifications requisite for Electors of the most numerous Branch of the State Legislature.

(2) No Person shall be a Representative who shall not have attained to the Age of twenty five Years, and been seven Years a Citizen of the United States, and who shall not, when elected, be an Inhabitant of that State in which he shall be chosen.

(3) ~~Representatives and direct Taxes shall be apportioned among the several States which may be included within this Union, according to their respective Numbers, which shall be determined by adding to the whole Number of free Persons, including those bound to Service for a Term of Years, and excluding Indians not taxed, three fifths of all other Persons.~~ The actual Enumeration shall be made within three Years after the first Meeting of the Congress of the United States, and within every subsequent Term of ten Years, in such Manner as they shall by Law direct. The Number of Representatives shall not exceed one for every thirty Thousand, but each State shall

have at Least one Representative; and until such enumeration shall be made, the State of New Hampshire shall be entitled to chuse three, Massachusetts eight, Rhode-Island and Providence Plantations one, Connecticut five, New-York six, New Jersey four, Pennsylvania eight, Delaware one, Maryland six, Virginia ten, North Carolina five, South Carolina five, and Georgia three.

(4) When vacancies happen in the Representation from any State, the Executive Authority thereof shall issue Writs of Election to fill such Vacancies.

(5) The House of Representatives shall chuse their Speaker and other Officers; and shall have the sole Power of Impeachment.

(1) *chosen . . . by the People of the several States*: The House of Representatives is the only federal body chosen directly by the people. But *which* people? For the most part, only free white males with property could vote—but the amount of property required for the franchise differed markedly from state to state, and any attempt to impose uniform standards would have encountered stiff resis-

tance. That is how our Constitution started. The Fifteenth, Nineteenth, Twenty-Fourth, and Twenty-Sixth Amendments would institute federal specifications that established a nearly universal franchise.

*every second Year*: Delegates to Congress under the Articles of Confederation had served one-year terms, but the demands on congressmen were now greater. Even so, compare a representative's two-year term with that of a senator or president. Frequent elections serve as the people's check on their representatives.

(2) *Age of twenty five Years . . . seven Years a Citizen of the United States . . . an Inhabitant of that State*: Note that the age and citizenship requirements for a representative are less stringent than the requirements for a senator (Article I, Section 3, Clause 3—thirty years old and nine years a citizen) or president (Article II, Section 1, Clause 5—thirty-five years old, a "natural born Citizen," and "fourteen Years a Resident within the United States").

(3) *Representatives . . . shall be apportioned among the several States . . . according to their respective Numbers*: Proportional representation for the House reflects national

citizenship: every person who is entitled to vote, regardless of the state of residence, has an equal voice. Every ten years an *enumeration* (census) determines the number of representatives for each state. But with no reliable census in 1787, the framers bickered over the initial allocation of representatives in this clause.

*three fifths of all other Persons*: Here is the Constitution's seamy underbelly. Southern delegates wanted to count the people whom they enslaved in the determination of how many representatives they had in Congress. "The labour of a slave in S. Carolina" was "as productive as that of a freeman in Massachusetts," observed Pierce Butler of South Carolina. But Pennsylvania's Gouverneur Morris countered: "Upon what principle is it that the slaves shall be computed in the representation? Are they men? Then make them citizens and let them vote. Are they property? Why then is no other property included?"

Four years earlier, in 1783, Congress had faced a similar situation when determining how much money each state should contribute to the federal treasury. At that time, to avoid paying extra money, *Southerners* maintained that slaves *should not* be counted, while *Northerners* thought that slaves *should* be counted because their labor provided wealth that needed to be included in any tally. Congress agreed in the end that each slave would count as three-fifths of a person. Although both sides reversed their positions between 1783 and 1787, delegates settled on the same fraction, three-fifths. There was no logic to that number. It was nothing more than a political calculation.

*The Number of Representatives shall not exceed one for every thirty Thousand*: On the last day of debates at the Constitutional Convention, George Washington made his one and only proposal: the standard should be one representative for every thirty thousand people, not one per forty thousand as stated in the almost-final draft. His idea was to tie representatives more closely to their constituencies. But as the population grew, the House expanded, and in 1929 Congress decided to cap the number of representatives at 435. As of May 2017, the resident population of the United States is approximately 326,200,000. Do the math: each representative now has some 749,885 constituents, hardly what Washington and the framers anticipated. On the other hand, if we stayed close to the ideal of one representative for every thirty thousand people, as Washington preferred, the House would have 10,873 members, not a workable body.

(4) *Election to fill such Vacancies*: Since each state has the right to full representation, vacancies must be filled in a timely manner.

(5) *the sole Power of Impeachment*: To "impeach" is to charge. The House initiates impeachment proceedings. The rest of the process is laid out in Article I, Section 3, Clause 6 and Article II, Section 4.

## SECTION. 3.

**(1) The Senate of the United States shall be composed of two Senators from each State, ~~chosen by the Legislature thereof,~~ for six Years; and each Senator shall have one Vote.**

**(2) Immediately after they shall be assembled in Consequence of the first Election, they shall be divided as equally as may be into three Classes. The Seats of the Senators of the first Class shall be vacated at the Expiration of the second Year, of the second Class at the Expiration of the fourth Year, and of the third Class at the Expiration of the sixth Year, so that one third may**

be chosen every second Year; ~~and if Vacancies happen by Resignation, or otherwise, during the Recess of the Legislature of any State, the Executive thereof may make temporary Appointments until the next Meeting of the Legislature, which shall then fill such Vacancies.~~

(3) No Person shall be a Senator who shall not have attained to the Age of thirty Years, and been nine Years a Citizen of the United States, and who shall not, when elected, be an Inhabitant of that State for which he shall be chosen.

(4) The Vice President of the United States shall be President of the Senate, but shall have no Vote, unless they be equally divided.

(5) The Senate shall chuse their other Officers, and also a President pro tempore, in the Absence of the Vice President, or when he shall exercise the Office of President of the United States.

(6) The Senate shall have the sole Power to try all Impeachments. When sitting for that Purpose, they shall be on Oath or Affir-

mation. **When the President of the United States is tried, the Chief Justice shall preside: And no Person shall be convicted without the Concurrence of two thirds of the Members present.**

**(7) Judgment in Cases of Impeachment shall not extend further than to removal from Office, and disqualification to hold and enjoy any Office of honor, Trust or Profit under the United States: but the Party convicted shall nevertheless be liable and subject to Indictment, Trial, Judgment and Punishment, according to Law.**

(1) *two Senators from each State*: The Virginia Plan, which served as the opening draft for the new Constitution, called for proportional representation in both houses of Congress, but small states, which would have little say under that arrangement, wanted states to vote equally in both houses. That was how Congress under the Articles of Confederation conducted business, and the sitting convention followed suit: one vote for each state, whether large or small. The framers finally settled on proportional representation in the House and equal representation in the Senate—the so-called Great Compro-

mise. While the Three-Fifths Compromise seems morally reprehensible today, the Great Compromise is lauded.

*chosen by the Legislature thereof*: Not until 1913, with passage of the Seventeenth Amendment, were citizens allowed to vote for their senators.

*for six Years*: Senators only have to stand for reelection every six years—less often than the president. The framers wanted to protect this deliberative body from public opinion and outside influence, much as their own convention had been shielded. (In fact, ten of the twenty senators in the First Federal Congress had helped write the Constitution.) During the ratification debates, opponents of the proposed Constitution objected to this elite legislative body, which was removed from the people yet vested with powers not shared by the House of Representatives (see Article II, Section 2, Clause 2).

(2) *divided as equally as may be into three Classes*: This rotation, with only one-third of the senators standing for election every two years, ensures continuity.

(3) *Age of thirty Years . . . nine Years a Citizen of the United States . . . Inhabitant of that*

*State for which he shall be chosen*: Senators must be older (and presumably wiser) than representatives. The citizenship requirement is also set higher.

(4) *Vice President . . . shall be President of the Senate*: The office of the vice president was a late entry, recommended to the Convention by a committee less than two weeks before adjournment. All the drafts until that moment stipulated that the president would be selected by Congress— and if a president died or could no longer serve, Congress would simply choose a new one. But the new and complex scheme of presidential electors (see Article II, Section 1, Clauses 2 and 3) required electors to select two people, with the second-place finisher becoming the president's successor. What was the vice president to do while he waited for the president to die? That he was to preside over the Senate raised eyebrows back then, as it does now. Technically, when Vice President Dick Cheney claimed to be part of the legislative branch, not the executive branch, he was correct. Only with time did the vice president assume executive duties not specified in the Constitution.

(5) *President pro tempore*: Quick quiz, without googling: Who is the current "President pro tempore" of the Senate? Anyone who can answer correctly is in a distinct minority. More people are likely to identify the Senate majority leader, who in fact wields far greater power, yet that politicized position goes unmentioned in the Constitution. The framers worried about "factions," but they did not foresee that the leader of one party would rise above the leader of the Senate as a whole.

(6) *Senate shall have the sole Power to try all Impeachments*: If the House impeaches a federal officer, the Senate determines whether that person should be removed from office. Two presidents—Andrew Johnson and Bill Clinton—have been tried, but neither was convicted. (Richard Nixon, who likely would have been convicted for the Watergate cover-up, resigned before the House could impeach him.) Eight federal judges have been impeached, convicted, and thereby removed from office.

*When the President of the United States is tried, the Chief Justice shall preside*: The vice president cannot preside over a trial that might result in making him president.

(7) *Judgment . . . shall not extend further than to removal from Office*: The Senate is not a judicial body. It can determine if a person is fit for office, but criminal allegations must be tried in a court of law.

## SECTION. 4.

**(1) The Times, Places and Manner of holding Elections for Senators and Representatives, shall be prescribed in each State by the Legislature thereof; but the Congress may at any time by Law make or alter such Regulations, except as to the Places of chusing Senators.**

**(2) The Congress shall assemble at least once in every Year, and such Meeting shall be on ~~the first Monday in December,~~ unless they shall by Law appoint a different Day.**

(1) *Times, Places and Manner of holding Elections*: The election process reflects the overall approach of the framers: states act on matters that affect them, but Congress can have the final say. Although the Constitution does not explicitly state who gets to construct congressional districts, "the Manner of holding elections" has historically included this authority. Every ten years (see

Article I, Section 2, Clause 3), each state legislature determines how to draw district lines. Although this provision is politically neutral, it has been applied to partisan advantage. After losing the presidency and both houses of Congress in 2008, Republican strategists focused on state governments, the majority then controlled by Democrats. The election of 2010—a census year—flipped numerous statehouses, and Republican-controlled legislatures redrew district lines to their advantage. The result: in 2012, Democratic candidates for the House of Representatives received 1.4 million more votes than Republicans, yet Republicans wound up with a thirty-three-member edge over their rivals. Had Democrats been in control in 2010, they undoubtedly would have drawn the lines to their advantage. Political alert: pay attention to state races in 2020, which will have huge consequences for the following decade.

(2) *Congress shall assemble at least once in every Year*: In pre-Revolutionary times, Crown-appointed royal governors had refused to convene colonial legislatures. Never again would legislators be prevented from showing up to work.

## SECTION. 5.

(1) Each House shall be the Judge of the Elections, Returns and Qualifications of its own Members, and a Majority of each shall constitute a Quorum to do Business; but a smaller Number may adjourn from day to day, and may be authorized to compel the Attendance of absent Members, in such Manner, and under such Penalties as each House may provide.

(2) Each House may determine the Rules of its Proceedings, punish its Members for disorderly Behaviour, and, with the Concurrence of two thirds, expel a Member.

(3) Each House shall keep a Journal of its Proceedings, and from time to time publish the same, excepting such Parts as may in their Judgment require Secrecy; and the Yeas and Nays of the Members of either House on any question shall, at the Desire of one fifth of those Present, be entered on the Journal.

(4) Neither House, during the Session of Congress, shall, without the Consent of the other, adjourn for more than three days,

**nor to any other Place than that in which
the two Houses shall be sitting.**

(1) *a Majority of each shall constitute a Quorum*: Without a quorum, a small minority might rule the day.

*may be authorized to compel the Attendance of absent Members*: A quorum requirement is subject to abuse. If attendance is weak for some reason, opponents of a measure that is likely to pass can simply not show up, denying a quorum. The framers were aware of this political trick and protected against it.

(2) *Each House may determine the Rules of its Proceedings*: This clause underscores the separation of powers: one chamber of Congress has no say in how the other conducts its business, nor can the executive or judicial branch intervene. In the House of Representatives, the Rules Committee sets time limits for all debates, but in the Senate one member can speak indefinitely, then yield the floor to a colleague who does the same. How can this "filibuster" be terminated? In 1917, the Senate decided that two-thirds of the members present could achieve "cloture," and in 1949, that threshold was changed to three-

fifths of all members, whether present or not. Since that time, complex rules governing the filibuster and cloture have been altered several times. Can the Senate consider another bill while a filibuster is happening? Can senators simply announce their intention to filibuster without having to talk nonstop? Can the threshold for cloture be reduced to a simple majority when considering a nomination? What should be the threshold for cloture when debating a change to the rules themselves? Only the Senate can decide such matters.

Some argue that requiring a supermajority for cloture is unconstitutional. Because the Constitution stipulates a supermajority for treaty ratifications, veto overrides, and impeachment convictions, we might infer that a simple majority should suffice for all other matters. The Supreme Court could not make that determination, however, without explicitly contradicting the fundamental premise of this clause.

(3) *Each House shall keep a Journal*: Transparency was as critical then as it is now. In a nation based on popular sovereignty, people must know what their government is doing to keep it in line.

(4) *Neither House . . . shall, without the Consent of the other, adjourn for more than three days*: The framers valued efficiency, and for Congress to get anything done, both houses have to meet at the same time. But Congress has discovered a way to bypass this constitutional obligation. If one house wants to adjourn while the other does not, it stages a bare-bones "pro forma" session without conducting any meaningful business.

*nor to any other Place other than that in which the two Houses shall be sitting*: Separation by distance would not present a problem now, but it did back then.

### SECTION. 6.

**(1) The Senators and Representatives shall receive a Compensation for their Services, to be ascertained by Law, and paid out of the Treasury of the United States. They shall in all Cases, except Treason, Felony and Breach of the Peace, be privileged from Arrest during their Attendance at the Session of their respective Houses, and in going to and returning from the same; and for any Speech or Debate in either House, they shall not be questioned in any other Place.**

**(2) No Senator or Representative shall, during the Time for which he was elected, be appointed to any civil Office under the Authority of the United States, which shall have been created, or the Emoluments whereof shall have been encreased during such time; and no Person holding any Office under the United States, shall be a Member of either House during his Continuance in Office.**

(1) *privileged from Arrest during their Attendance at the Session*: Imagine otherwise— a cop stops a senator or representative for an alleged traffic violation to prevent the driver from casting a particular vote. That can't happen here.

(2) *No Senator or Representative shall . . . be appointed to any civil Office . . . which shall have been created, or the Emoluments whereof shall have been encreased during such time*: This clause prevents senators or representatives from creating jobs for themselves or increasing remuneration for posts they expect to occupy. This can be problematic, however. During Hillary Clinton's term as senator for New York, Congress increased the salary of the secretary of state. Clinton

had no designs on that office; instead, she was planning a run for the presidency at the time. Then, after President Obama made her secretary of state, Congress reduced the office's salary to its original level so that Clinton would not materially benefit from the pay hike—the *spirit* of this constitutional provision. Even so, according to the *letter* of the law, Clinton should have been ineligible for the office of secretary of state. (Clinton was only the latest, not the first, to run into this constitutional conundrum.) Should we turn a blind eye to the spirit of the Constitution in order to support its letter, or vice versa? Legal experts have oscillated on this particular issue over the years. It is not settled law.

*No Senator or Representative shall, during the Time for which he was elected, be appointed to any civil Office*: The framers wanted to decentralize authority. Holding multiple offices had been greatly abused during colonial rule, concentrating power in the hands of a few.

### SECTION. 7.

**(1) All Bills for raising Revenue shall originate in the House of Representatives; but the Senate may propose or concur with Amendments as on other Bills.**

**(2)** Every Bill which shall have passed the House of Representatives and the Senate, shall, before it becomes a Law, be presented to the President of the United States; If he approve he shall sign it, but if not he shall return it, with his Objections to that House in which it shall have originated, who shall enter the Objections at large on their Journal, and proceed to reconsider it. If after such Reconsideration two thirds of that House shall agree to pass the Bill, it shall be sent, together with the Objections, to the other House, by which it shall likewise be reconsidered, and if approved by two thirds of that House, it shall become a Law. But in all such Cases the Votes of both Houses shall be determined by yeas and Nays, and the Names of the Persons voting for and against the Bill shall be entered on the Journal of each House respectively. If any Bill shall not be returned by the President within ten Days (Sundays excepted) after it shall have been presented to him, the Same shall be a Law, in like Manner as if he had signed it, unless the Congress by their Adjournment prevent its Return, in which Case it shall not be a Law.

**(3)** Every Order, Resolution, or Vote to which the Concurrence of the Senate and

**House of Representatives may be necessary (except on a question of Adjournment) shall be presented to the President of the United States; and before the Same shall take Effect, shall be approved by him, or being disapproved by him, shall be repassed by two thirds of the Senate and House of Representatives, according to the Rules and Limitations prescribed in the Case of a Bill.**

(1) *All Bills for raising Revenue shall originate in the House of Representatives*: This provision, championed by Benjamin Franklin, is an overlooked part of the Great Compromise. With all the fuss in Revolutionary times about "no taxation without representation," Franklin and others wanted to make sure that any taxes were initiated by the people's direct representatives.

*the Senate may propose or concur with Amendments*: Since most bills are amended numerous times by each house and then in a joint committee to resolve any differences, the stipulation that revenue bills originate in the House was "politically correct" for those times but of little import now.

(2) and (3) *If he approve he shall sign it, but if not he shall return it*: The presidential veto (what the framers called a "negative") is a signature component of checks and balances: a president can check Congress by vetoing any measure that both houses have approved, but Congress, with a two-thirds majority of each house, can override the president's veto. The framers loved the basic idea but had a difficult time settling on the supermajority required for a congressional override. They started with two-thirds, changed midstream to three-quarters, and then, just days before they adjourned, switched back to two-thirds. In practice, Congress has found it difficult to clear the two-thirds hurdle. It overrode a presidential veto only once in the first sixty-five years and has overridden only 4 percent of all presidential vetoes.

## SECTION. 8.

(1) The Congress shall have Power To lay and collect Taxes, Duties, Imposts and Excises, to pay the Debts and provide for the common Defence and general Welfare of the United States; but all Duties, Imposts and Excises shall be uniform throughout the United States;

**(2)** To borrow Money on the credit of the United States;

**(3)** To regulate Commerce with foreign Nations, and among the several States, and with the Indian Tribes;

**(4)** To establish an uniform Rule of Naturalization, and uniform Laws on the subject of Bankruptcies throughout the United States;

**(5)** To coin Money, regulate the Value thereof, and of foreign Coin, and fix the Standard of Weights and Measures;

**(6)** To provide for the Punishment of counterfeiting the Securities and current Coin of the United States;

**(7)** To establish Post Offices and post Roads;

**(8)** To promote the Progress of Science and useful Arts, by securing for limited Times to Authors and Inventors the exclusive Right to their respective Writings and Discoveries;

(9) To constitute Tribunals inferior to the supreme Court;

(10) To define and punish Piracies and Felonies committed on the high Seas, and Offences against the Law of Nations;

(11) To declare War, grant Letters of Marque and Reprisal, and make Rules concerning Captures on Land and Water;

(12) To raise and support Armies, but no Appropriation of Money to that Use shall be for a longer Term than two Years;

(13) To provide and maintain a Navy;

(14) To make Rules for the Government and Regulation of the land and naval Forces;

(15) To provide for calling forth the Militia to execute the Laws of the Union, suppress Insurrections and repel Invasions;

(16) To provide for organizing, arming, and disciplining, the Militia, and for governing such Part of them as may be employed in the Service of the United States, reserving

to the States respectively, the Appointment of the Officers, and the Authority of training the Militia according to the discipline prescribed by Congress;

(17) To exercise exclusive Legislation in all Cases whatsoever, over such District (not exceeding ten Miles square) as may, by Cession of particular States, and the Acceptance of Congress, become the Seat of the Government of the United States, and to exercise like Authority over all Places purchased by the Consent of the Legislature of the State in which the Same shall be, for the Erection of Forts, Magazines, Arsenals, dock-Yards, and other needful Buildings;—And

(18) To make all Laws which shall be necessary and proper for carrying into Execution the foregoing Powers, and all other Powers vested by this Constitution in the Government of the United States, or in any Department or Officer thereof.

Article I, Section 8 is the meat of the Constitution. Although the president enforces the laws, Congress has to make them first, and here is where the legislative powers of the federal government are spelled out. But are some powers *implied* by those specifically *enumerated*? Responses to this question have led to heated political debates since the 1790s, when Secretary of the Treasury Alexander Hamilton proposed a national bank. Was that constitutional, even though no such power was specifically listed? Keep this question in mind as you examine the eighteen enumerated powers.

(1) *To lay and collect Taxes*: To taxes we owe our Constitution. Congress's inability to raise money on its own had killed the Articles of Confederation. In reaction, first and foremost, the framers granted Congress broad powers of taxation. Note the sweeping language: *to pay the Debts and provide for the common Defence and general Welfare*. All taxes, save on exports (see Article I, Section 9, Clause 5), are fair game, but there are two restrictions on the *manner* of taxation: *Duties, Imposts and Excises shall be uniform,* and direct taxes must be proportional to state populations (see Article I, Section 9, Clause 4).

(2) *To borrow Money*: Taxes make Congress solvent in the long term, but what if the nation is invaded and money is needed instantly? The framers viewed the unre-

stricted authority to borrow money as critical to national defense. They did not envision permanent debt of major proportions, but neither did they prohibit it. In fact, Alexander Hamilton and others believed that a national debt could be beneficial because it gave those who held government securities a vested stake in the solvency of the nation.

(3) *To regulate Commerce with foreign Nations, and among the several States*: The commerce clause is the most litigated provision in the original body of the Constitution. In 1787, commerce meant trade—mostly maritime, since overland trade over long distances was cumbersome and trading partners were primarily overseas. Trade items were limited: regional crops and resources such as tobacco, rice, wheat, and timber shipped outward, while manufactured goods from Europe, sugar from the West Indies, and slaves from Africa came here. Today, interstate and international commerce includes practically everything, save for farmers' markets and local service sector activities. The vast majority of traded goods are shipped from foreign nations or other states, and goods produced locally will find homes elsewhere. So how do we apply this provision now?

The big question: How broad is the term *Commerce*? Does that cover only the movement of goods, or can it apply to goods that are moved? Can the conditions and pay of workers who make these goods be addressed under this clause since without workers there would be no goods to trade? Can services that are not strictly local be covered as well as goods?

Supreme Court decisions have varied generation to generation. In the 1930s, the court struck down several New Deal statutes that based their authority on the commerce clause, but in 1941, it upheld the Fair Labor Standards Act, which mandated the forty-hour workweek. In 1964, the court upheld an act banning racial discrimination in hotels and restaurants that served customers from out of state. But in 2012, a 5–4 majority determined that the Affordable Care Act could not be based on interstate commerce, even though the health-care industry accounts for 17 percent of the gross domestic product. (It did, however, uphold the law based on Congress's power to tax.) Look for the pendulum to swing—or not—depending on upcoming appointments to the court.

*and with the Indian Tribes*: Previously, under the Articles of Confederation, individual states dealt separately with Indian nations.

(4) *uniform Rule of Naturalization*: The Constitution does not define citizenship here. That would come in Section 1 of the Fourteenth Amendment.

*uniform Laws on the subject of Bankruptcies*: Why are *Naturalization* and *Bankruptcies* linked in the same sentence? The key word here is *uniform.* State-by-state variations for either would be chaotic.

(5) *To coin Money . . . and fix the Standard of Weights and Measures*: These, too, must not vary by state. But in the spirit of uniformity, why has Congress not switched to the metric system? Here is American exceptionalism in action. Only Myanmar (Burma) and Liberia are with us on that score.

(6) *Punishment of counterfeiting*: Counterfeiting would seem to be covered under the preceding clause, but here the framers authorize Congress to punish offenders. The practice had been a scourge in Revolutionary times.

(7) *Post Offices and post Roads*: Postal service was key to forming a nation from disparate states. Post riders carried not only letters but also newspapers across post roads, which

connected distant towns and had fewer ruts, rocks, and potholes than other roads. What are today's equivalent of post roads, linking American citizens through the exchange of information? Airwaves and the Internet (think net neutrality) are surely worthy of federal attention.

(8) *the exclusive Right to their respective Writings and Discoveries*: Protection of intellectual property rights, central to entrepreneurship, was alive and well at the nation's founding. But note the qualification: *limited Times.* Pay attention, Big Pharma: the right to commandeer scientific progress for private gain is not guaranteed by the Constitution.

(9) *Tribunals inferior to the supreme Court*: Wisely, the framers did not construct a complete edifice for the judicial department. Needs would vary with national expansion, so they left the matter to future Congresses.

(10) *punish Piracies*: In the eighteenth century, both pirates and counterfeiters (recall Clause 6) presented threats to national security—the first interfering with international trade, the second endangering the value of money.

*Offences against the Law of Nations*: This refers to general principles summarized in a book by the Swiss philosopher Emer de Vattel, read by several framers. They expected the United States to assume its place among nations, abiding by basic moral principles—today, think international law and the Geneva Accords.

(11) *declare War*: Only Congress, not the president, can commit American blood and treasure to a significant conflict. The Committee of Detail draft, prepared after two months of deliberations, authorized Congress to "make war," but some delegates worried that if Congress was not in session, the nation would be unable to respond to an attack quickly enough. In this case, the president could "make war," at least until Congress was back in session and could decide whether to "declare war," as authorized in this clause.

That is how it was supposed to work, but the last time Congress declared war was in 1941. Wars in Korea, Vietnam, Iraq, and Afghanistan were all undeclared. Now, with ISIS and terrorism generally, there is not even a nation-state to declare war *against*. How, then, do we apply Article I, Section 8,

Clause 11? This is indeed problematic, legally and politically. If one party controls Congress and the other the presidency, we can readily surmise which party will be promoting the primacy of each branch.

*grant Letters of Marque and Reprisal*: These permit armed private vessels ("privateers") to prey on enemy merchant ships with the government sharing the spoils. This was legalized piracy, recognized at the time by international law. The Revolutionary War was financed in large measure by the government's take from privateering. If the militia was the people's army, privateers functioned as the people's navy. In 1856, when European powers banned privateering, the United States refused to sign on. Note that the authority to grant letters of marque and reprisal appears proximate to declaring war, the first in a cluster of six critical clauses dealing with military matters.

(12), (13), and (14) *raise and support Armies . . . provide and maintain a Navy . . . Regulation of the land and naval Forces*: It seems obvious to us: Congress must have the power to create armed forces. At the time, however, this was a contentious issue. The British military presence in America, which

helped spark the Revolutionary War, continued to rankle. Would a standing army, even
in peacetime, present a threat to America's
liberty? On the other hand, could the nation
survive without one?

*no Appropriation of Money . . . for a
longer Term than two Years*: When George
Washington retired from service after the
Revolutionary War, he pushed for a "proper
Peace Establishment," asking for a standing
army without using those provocative words.
The framers, likewise, did what they could
to sweeten the deal. By imposing a two-year
limit, they allowed the people's representatives to keep tabs on the military and cut off
funds if need be.

Understandably absent from this clause is
any mention of an air force. If enumerated
powers are treated strictly by the letter of the
law, Congress would not be authorized to
raise and sustain an air force. Here is a text-
book case of an implied power: military bodies back then were limited to *land and naval
Forces,* but these can be viewed as stand-ins
for other military bodies the framers had
not envisioned—an air force now, perhaps
a space force in time. For the Constitution
to remain relevant, it must be interpreted in
ways that make sense in the present.

(15) and (16) *calling forth the Militia . . . orga-nizing, arming, and disciplining, the Militia*: The preferred alternative to a standing army was the militia, seen as the military embodiment of the people. Militia units during the Revolutionary War had mixed records, but at times, such as the capture of Burgoyne's army at Saratoga, they proved invaluable. However, local militia had failed to suppress the insurrection in Massachusetts, largely because many militiamen sided with the rebels. With these two provisions, Congress would be able to place militia in the national service, reserving to the states only the training and choice of officers.

(17) *exercise exclusive Legislation . . . over . . . the Seat of the Government*: If the nation's capital lay within a state, that state could exercise some control over federal officials. In the new government, however, federal trumped state—more of this in Article VI. The capital, therefore, should be its own unique city, under the thumb of Congress.

Where might the capital be located? New York and Philadelphia, the two temporary locations, lay in the middle states and would seem likely candidates, but Southerners had traveled north since the First Continental

Congress met in Philadelphia in 1774. In 1790, supposedly over dinner, Thomas Jefferson, James Madison, and Alexander Hamilton brokered a deal. Congressmen from districts bordering the Potomac River would support Hamilton's plan for the federal assumption of state war debts; in return, they got the nation's capital.

One problem remained: Would residents of the national capital, stateless, have any voice in the federal government? Check out the Twenty-Third Amendment and its limitations.

(18) *make all Laws which shall be necessary and proper for carrying into Execution the foregoing Powers*: Even though this clause was admittedly sweeping and singularly different from the others, it caused no stir, discussion, or debate at the Constitutional Convention. The framers viewed this measure as an essential complement to the rest. Without it, administration of all the other powers might be compromised. We now call it the "elastic" clause, but just how far should it stretch?

Let's return now to Hamilton's national bank, which Congress approved early in 1791. President Washington liked the idea, but he noted that the United States Constitution did not specifically authorize the federal government to charter banks. This presented a dilemma: Should he sign the bill that Congress had sent him, which he believed would help the nation, or should he veto it because it exerted powers not *explicitly* authorized by the Constitution?

Washington asked his attorney general, Edmund Randolph, for a legal opinion, and Randolph gave a decisive answer: no specific clause in the Constitution empowered Congress to incorporate a national bank. If "necessary and proper" were given too great a "latitude," it would be subject to dangerous abuse and "terminate in an unlimited power in Congress."

Washington saw Randolph's point, and he asked his close friend and political confidant James Madison, who had opposed the bill in the House of Representatives, to draft a veto message. Madison's draft stated point-blank: "I object to the Bill because it is an essential principle of the Government that powers not delegated by the Constitution cannot be rightfully exercised; because the power proposed by the bill to be received is not expressly delegated; and because I cannot satisfy myself that it results from any express power by fair and safe rules of implication."

Before delivering that message, Washington asked Hamilton to respond to the arguments proffered by the bank's opponents. "Every power vested in a government," Hamilton proclaimed, "includes . . . a right to employ all the *means* requisite, and *fairly applicable* to the attainment of the *ends* of such power, and which are not precluded by restrictions and exceptions specified in the Constitution, or not immoral, or not contrary to the ends of political society." Congress was empowered to raise money, and it was charged with protecting the nation. Suppose the nation were threatened by a foreign power, he conjectured. Raising the money by taxes would take too long, but "if there be a bank the supply can at once be had." A national bank was a practical means of "raising and supporting" an army in case of emergency—and that power *was* granted to Congress. It was, he concluded, an implied power.

In the end, whether right or wrong, the president sided with Hamilton. Washington had been pushing for a strong, efficient national government for years, and a veto based on a limited interpretation of the "necessary and proper" powers of Congress would have ceded much of the ground he and his fellow nationalists had gained by framing, ratifying, and implementing the Constitution. It was a truly momentous decision. Had Washington declared for the other side, the entire trajectory of the federal government would likely have been altered.

Today, we still quarrel over "strict" versus "broad" constructions of the Constitution, much as Americans did in the 1790s. We do so because the Constitution signals mixed messages, and that is neither an accident nor a mistake. The framers refused to declare unfalteringly for "strict" or "broad" because either choice, unmodified, would have been untenable. Without enumerating powers, the Constitution would permit the indefinite expansion of federal authority, yet without the flexibility inherent in implied powers, Congress could allocate no funds to provide for even minimal airport security, monitor weather to warn people of hurricanes, finance research for curing cancer, or allocate funds once every four years for inauguration ceremonies. Admittedly, *all* would not be lost. Even now, under Article I, Section 8, Clauses 10 and 11, Congress would still possess the authority to "punish Piracies" and "grant Letters of Marque and Reprisal."

## SECTION. 9.

(1) The Migration or Importation of such Persons as any of the States now existing shall think proper to admit, shall not be prohibited by the Congress prior to the Year one thousand eight hundred and eight, but a Tax or duty may be imposed on such Importation, not exceeding ten dollars for each Person.

(2) The Privilege of the Writ of Habeas Corpus shall not be suspended, unless when in Cases of Rebellion or Invasion the public Safety may require it.

(3) No Bill of Attainder or ex post facto Law shall be passed.

(4) No Capitation, or other direct, Tax shall be laid, ~~unless in Proportion to the Census or enumeration herein before directed to be taken.~~

(5) No Tax or Duty shall be laid on Articles exported from any State.

(6) No Preference shall be given by any Regulation of Commerce or Revenue to the Ports of one State over those of another: nor

shall Vessels bound to, or from, one State, be obliged to enter, clear, or pay Duties in another.

(7) No Money shall be drawn from the Treasury, but in Consequence of Appropriations made by Law; and a regular Statement and Account of the Receipts and Expenditures of all public Money shall be published from time to time.

(8) No Title of Nobility shall be granted by the United States: And no Person holding any Office of Profit or Trust under them, shall, without the Consent of the Congress, accept of any present, Emolument, Office, or Title, of any kind whatever, from any King, Prince, or foreign State.

Having enumerated the powers of Congress in Section 8, the framers here forbid others. This would have been the perfect place for them to include a list of rights within the body of the Constitution, but they didn't do so. At the First Federal Congress almost two years later, when James Madison presented a list of amendments that protected rights, he suggested inserting most of them here. If Madison had had his way, what are now the

First through Sixth Amendments, and the Eighth Amendment, would be included in Article 1, Section 9. Instead, Connecticut's Roger Sherman convinced Congress to place what we now call the Bill of Rights at the end of the Constitution.

(1) *Importation of such Persons*: This meant slaves, but the framers shied from using that word. The political alignment that resulted in this provision was complex. Delegates from the Deep South (Georgia and South Carolina) feared that Congress would ban the importation of enslaved people from Africa, while delegates from the Upper South (Virginia and Maryland) favored a ban on slave importation. Why? Tobacco planters in the Upper South had a surfeit of slaves, some of whom they sold to western settlers. The Lower South's rice and indigo plantations required more slave labor than did tobacco plantations, so planters there replenished a workforce that perished from the sickly conditions in rice swamps. New England delegates, whose constituencies included a few slave-trading merchants, struck a deal with those of the Lower South: New England delegates would oppose a ban on slave importation, while Lower South delegates

would not push for a supermajority thresh-old on commerce legislation. The result: twenty more years of constitutionally sanc-tioned slave importation. Only then could the nation begin to wean itself of a practice that most framers believed was a national disgrace.

(2) *Writ of Habeas Corpus*: In Latin, "You may have the body." A person held in custody can demand that law-enforcement officials show a court cause for the detention.

(3) *Bill of Attainder*: A legislative act that pun-ishes a specific individual or group without trial.

   *ex post facto Law*: After-the-fact legisla-tion that criminalizes past actions.

(4) *No Capitation, or other direct, Tax . . . unless in Proportion to the Census*: A *Capi-tation Tax* (also known as a head tax or poll tax) is levied equally on each citizen no mat-ter how rich or poor. A *direct Tax* is levied directly on a person or property, as contrasted with an indirect tax, which is levied on an activity—typically importing or purchasing. Theoretically, an indirect tax is discretionary: a person can avoid it simply by not engaging

in that specific activity. Direct taxes, on the other hand, can't be avoided, so the framers placed a special restriction on them: each state must pay only its proportional share. (This is also stated in Article I, Section 2, Clause 3.) The framers worried, for example, that a federal tax on cultivated land would fall more heavily on regions in which farming was more intensive. By making direct taxes proportional, they hoped to avoid regional imbalance.

What about an income tax? Did the original Constitution permit it? The short answer is yes—the federal government levied income taxes long before passage of the Sixteenth Amendment in 1913. In dispute, however, was whether income taxes were direct, which had to be proportional, or indirect, which did not. The long answer will wait until we discuss that amendment.

(5) *No Tax or Duty . . . on Articles exported*: This is the only type of tax specifically prohibited by the Constitution. Several framers supported export taxes, but others argued that they are inherently unfair. An export tax on tobacco, for instance, would make Virginia planters assume more than their fair share of the tax burden.

(6) *No Preference . . . given . . . to the Ports of one State*: Congress must of course avoid regional bias.

*nor shall Vessels bound to, or from, one State be obliged to . . . pay Duties to another*: To facilitate interstate commerce, here is our own internal free trade agreement, embedded within the Constitution.

(7) *No Money shall be drawn from the Treasury, but in Consequence of Appropriations made by Law*: Congress must authorize all expenditures. The people's direct representatives are ultimately responsible for spending the people's money. In practice, though, Congress approves a budget but does not micromanage it. Executive department officials spend the *Appropriations made by Law.*

(8) *No Title of Nobility*: Alexander Hamilton referred to this provision as "the cornerstone of republican government." When a committee in the first Senate proposed to address the president as "His Highness the President of the United States of America, and Protector of their Liberties," opponents pointed to this clause in the Constitution. Even to hint at a *Title of Nobility* would not do.

*no Person holding any Office . . . shall,*

*without the consent of Congress, accept
of any present, Emolument, Office, or title, of
any kind whatever, from any King, Prince,
or foreign State*: The framers approved this
clause unanimously and without debate. Its
intent is clear: American officials cannot be
bought by foreign interests. The 2016 election of Donald Trump thrust this formerly
obscure clause into the limelight because of
the new president's global business interests.
If foreign leaders offer incentives or sweet-
heart deals to the Trump Organization, does
that constitute an *Emolument,* defined as
"an advantage, profit, or gain arising from
the possession of an office"?

This measure, carried over from the Articles of Confederation, was cast in uncharac-
teristically sweeping language: *of any kind
whatever.* (That is matched only in Article I,
Section 8, Clause 13, which grants Congress legislative authority over the District of
Columbia *in all Cases whatsoever.*) Typically,
to avoid even the appearance of conflicts of
interest, presidents have placed their business
ventures in blind trusts while in office, but if
a president refuses to do so, enforcement of
the Emoluments Clause is problematic. The
Supreme Court has determined that to establish standing for a legal suit, "a private indi-

vidual . . . must show . . . a direct injury . . . and it is not sufficient that he has merely a general interest common to all members of the public" (*Ex parte Levitt,* 1937). Perhaps a business rival of the Trump Organization could demonstrate financial harm, but what would be the appropriate legal remedy? This would lead to uncharted waters. Politically, the phrase *without the consent of Congress* might come into play. If members of Congress suspect that a president has received an emolument *of any kind whatever* from a *King, Prince, or foreign State,* it could demand a say in the matter. Here is one more instance of the Constitution's finely tuned system of checks and balances.

## SECTION. 10.

(1) No State shall enter into any Treaty, Alliance, or Confederation; grant Letters of Marque and Reprisal; coin Money; emit Bills of Credit; make any Thing but gold and silver Coin a Tender in Payment of Debts; pass any Bill of Attainder, ex post facto Law, or Law impairing the Obligation of Contracts, or grant any Title of Nobility.

(2) No State shall, without the Consent of the Congress, lay any Imposts or Duties

on Imports or Exports, except what may be absolutely necessary for executing it's inspection Laws: and the net Produce of all Duties and Imposts, laid by any State on Imports or Exports, shall be for the Use of the Treasury of the United States; and all such Laws shall be subject to the Revision and Controul of the Congress.

(3) No State shall, without the Consent of Congress, lay any Duty of Tonnage, keep Troops, or Ships of War in time of Peace, enter into any Agreement or Compact with another State, or with a foreign Power, or engage in War, unless actually invaded, or in such imminent Danger as will not admit of delay.

The various powers listed here are generally held by sovereign states. This section delineates ways in which states within the United States are *not* entirely sovereign.

(1) *No State shall . . . emit Bills of Credit; make any Thing but gold and silver Coin a Tender in Payment of Debts; . . . or Law impairing the Obligation of Contracts*: The framers targeted these restrictions because

state legislatures were passing such measures for debtor relief.

(2) *No State shall, without the Consent of the Congress, lay any Imposts or Duties on Imports or Exports . . . and the net Produce of all Duties and Imposts . . . shall be for the Use of the Treasury of the United States*: During the Confederation period, some states with ports financed their state governments by laying duties. Henceforth, only the federal government would benefit by duties.

(3) *No State shall . . . enter into any Agreement or Compact with another State, or with a foreign Power, or engage in War*: The bottom line: states cannot act like nations, nor can some states combine with others in compacts that might divide the United States.

## ARTICLE. II.

### SECTION. 1.

**(1) The executive Power shall be vested in a President of the United States of America. He shall hold his Office during the Term of four Years, and, together with the Vice**

President, chosen for the same Term, be elected, as follows

(2) Each State shall appoint, in such Manner as the Legislature thereof may direct, a Number of Electors, equal to the whole Number of Senators and Representatives to which the State may be entitled in the Congress: but no Senator or Representative, or Person holding an Office of Trust or Profit under the United States, shall be appointed an Elector.

(3) The Electors shall meet in their respective States, and vote by Ballot for two Persons, of whom one at least shall not be an Inhabitant of the same State with themselves. And they shall make a List of all the Persons voted for, and of the Number of Votes for each; which List they shall sign and certify, and transmit sealed to the Seat of the Government of the United States, directed to the President of the Senate. The President of the Senate shall, in the Presence of the Senate and House of Representatives, open all the Certificates, and the Votes shall then be counted. The Person having the greatest Number of Votes shall be the President, if such Number be

~~a Majority of the whole Number of Electors appointed; and if there be more than one who have such Majority, and have an equal Number of Votes, then the House of Representatives shall immediately chuse by Ballot one of them for President; and if no Person have a Majority, then from the five highest on the List the said House shall in like Manner chuse the President. But in chusing the President, the Votes shall be taken by States, the Representation from each State having one Vote; A quorum for this Purpose shall consist of a Member or Members from two thirds of the States, and a Majority of all the States shall be necessary to a Choice. In every Case, after the Choice of the President, the Person having the greatest Number of Votes of the Electors shall be the Vice President. But if there should remain two or more who have equal Votes, the Senate shall chuse from them by Ballot the Vice President.~~

(4) The Congress may determine the Time of chusing the Electors, and the Day on which they shall give their Votes; which Day shall be the same throughout the United States.

(5) No Person except a natural born Citizen, or a Citizen of the United States, at the time of the Adoption of this Constitution, shall be eligible to the Office of President; neither shall any Person be eligible to that Office who shall not have attained to the Age of thirty five Years, and been fourteen Years a Resident within the United States.

(6) ~~In Case of the Removal of the President from Office, or of his Death, Resignation, or Inability to discharge the Powers and Duties of the said Office, the Same shall devolve on the Vice President, and the Congress may by Law provide for the Case of Removal, Death, Resignation or Inability, both of the President and Vice President, declaring what Officer shall then act as President, and such Officer shall act accordingly, until the Disability be removed, or a President shall be elected.~~

(7) The President shall, at stated Times, receive for his Services, a Compensation, which shall neither be encreased nor diminished during the Period for which he shall have been elected, and he shall not receive within that Period any other Emol-

**ument from the United States, or any of them.**

**(8) Before he enter on the Execution of his Office, he shall take the following Oath or Affirmation:—"I do solemnly swear (or affirm) that I will faithfully execute the Office of President of the United States, and will to the best of my Ability, preserve, protect and defend the Constitution of the United States."**

On April 16, 1787, shortly before the framers met in Philadelphia, James Madison wrote to George Washington about the need for a national government with broad authorities, including "a negative [veto] *in all cases whatsoever* on the legislative acts of the States." But "a Government composed of such extensive powers should be well organized and balanced," he wrote. To this end, Madison offered specific ideas for a bicameral national legislature and a national judiciary, but here is all he had to say about the executive branch: "A national Executive must also be provided. I have scarcely ventured as yet to form my own opinion either of the manner in which it ought to be constituted or of the authorities with which it ought to be cloathed."

Little wonder Madison stumbled over the executive. On the one hand, Americans at the time wanted no part of a monarchy, but on the other, executive functions during the Confederation were performed by committee, and that proved woefully inadequate. The framers had to walk a fine line. If a single executive too closely resembled a king, might a plural executive, perhaps three leaders, be better than one? How might he or they be chosen? (They did not imagine a "she.") How long might he or they serve? Should he or they be eligible for reelection? Could he or they be removed from office, and if so, by whom and for what reasons? And most of all: What powers might an executive have in a republic grounded on popular sovereignty?

(1) *President of the United States of America*: The framers settled quickly on a single executive, whom they decided to call the president.

*four Years*: The framers considered terms of three, four, seven, eight, fifteen, and twenty years, as well as "during good behavior," which meant indefinitely. To keep the president somewhat accountable and to avoid the appearance of a monarchy, they rejected the longer terms. They placed no limits on the number of terms a president can serve—

that would come with the Twenty-Second Amendment, ratified in 1951.

(2), (3), and (4) *Each State shall appoint . . . a Number of Electors*: Here is the simplest possible explanation of a ridiculously complex method for choosing the president. Each state legislature chooses in any manner it wishes (by popular vote or the legislature; by districts or statewide) a number of electors equal to the total number of members that state has in Congress (House + Senate). Electors cannot hold other public offices. Meeting in their respective states, each elector votes for two people, but at least one must be from another state. The person receiving the most votes is president and the runner-up vice president. If nobody receives a majority, the House of Representatives chooses the president from among the top five candidates. The runner-up in the House runoff is vice president. Voting in the House is by state delegations. (Small states refused to go along with the electoral system unless each state had an equal say in the runoff.)

Why such an arrangement, original and untested? The framers considered two other options, each with its problems.

For most of the Convention, they figured

the president would be chosen by Congress, much as Parliament chooses its prime minister. But if the president is a creature of Congress, how can he be independent of Congress?

A small minority wanted the people to elect the president, but this was rejected soundly three times. Most framers did not think the people could be trusted with such a momentous decision. "It would be as unnatural to refer the choice of a proper character for chief Magistrate to the people," George Mason declared, "as it would, to refer a trial of colours to a blind man."

Late in the proceedings, with less than two weeks before adjournment, a committee came up with the ingenious system of presidential electors. Because electors were not part of any government and met separately, they would be removed from political intrigue. Chosen for their greater wisdom, they would supposedly exercise individual discretion and cast their votes for the best person, free of all bias.

It hasn't worked out that way. When competing political parties emerged in the 1790s, each party put forth a set of electors pledged to its preferred candidate. Electors ever since have been mere placeholders, which has undermined the whole purpose of the framers' creative system. Only recently have more than one or two "faithless" electors refused to cast votes for the standard-bearer of their party. In 2016, two Republican electors pledged to Donald Trump did not vote for him, while five Democrats rejected Hillary Clinton. (Three other electors tried to buck their party's nominee, but officials managed to replace them.) Constitutionally speaking, faithless electors, entirely unknown to the voters who chose them, could change the outcome of a close presidential election.

Political operatives figured out how to game the elector process in the first contested presidential election (1796), and by the election of 1800, the system imploded. That led to the Twelfth Amendment, which solved only one of several problems. More on that soon.

Because the framers opted for an elector system rather than direct voting by the people, five candidates who prevailed in the popular vote have "lost" the election for president: Andrew Jackson in 1824, Samuel Tilden in 1876, Grover Cleveland in 1888, Al Gore in 2000, and Hillary Clinton in 2016.

(5) *natural born Citizen*: This has caused considerable confusion. In legal terms, there are

two ways to interpret "natural born citizen": *jus soli* ("right of the soil," meaning born in the country) and *jus sanguinis* ("right of blood," meaning born to parents who are citizens). Which method is enshrined in the United States Constitution? The records of the Constitutional Convention say nothing about this. Other records from the time are mixed: Madison in 1789 said that "place is the most certain criterion," but the following year Congress enacted legislation stating that children of United States citizens born overseas were natural born citizens. Was Ted Cruz, a 2016 candidate for president with an American mother and Canadian father, a natural born citizen? Or was John McCain, the 2008 Republican nominee who was born in the Panama Canal Zone, a natural born citizen? Place or parentage, which is it? Scholars and others argue the case on both sides with great certainty, but we can only speculate, no more than that. Perhaps it was a soupy mix of the two, no clearer then than now.

*Age of thirty five Years*: Monarchs and titled nobility can assume their positions when not yet mature—but nothing like that should happen here. No child of a popular president can be elected to that office before fully matured.

*fourteen Years a Resident within the United States*: Natural born citizen is not enough; a lengthy presence is also required.

(6) *shall devolve on the Vice President*: Does that mean the vice president becomes president for the remainder of the four-year term, or does he merely assume the *Powers and Duties* of the presidency until a new election can be held? This ambiguous first draft at presidential succession was clarifed by the Twenty-Fifth Amendment.

(7) *Compensation, which shall neither be encreased nor diminished*: If Congress could raise or lower a sitting president's salary, it would undermine the independence of that office.

*any other Emolument from the United States, or any of them*: This prevents Congress or a state from currying the president's favor through gifts.

(8) *Oath or Affirmation:—"I do solemnly swear (or affirm)"*: The option to *affirm* acknowledges religious groups opposed to swearing an oath. Note, too, the absence of "so help me God"—an addition that some say, without contemporaneous evidence,

started with Washington. (There is no record from the time that any of the first fifteen presidents used this phrase.) Article VI, Section 3, prohibits a "religious Test" for any federal office.

### SECTION. 2.

(1) The President shall be Commander in Chief of the Army and Navy of the United States, and of the Militia of the several States, when called into the actual Service of the United States; he may require the Opinion, in writing, of the principal Officer in each of the executive Departments, upon any Subject relating to the Duties of their respective Offices, and he shall have Power to grant Reprieves and Pardons for Offences against the United States, except in Cases of Impeachment.

(2) He shall have Power, by and with the Advice and Consent of the Senate, to make Treaties, provided two thirds of the Senators present concur; and he shall nominate, and by and with the Advice and Consent of the Senate, shall appoint Ambassadors, other public Ministers and Consuls, Judges of the supreme Court, and all other Officers of the United States,

whose Appointments are not herein otherwise provided for, and which shall be established by Law: but the Congress may by Law vest the Appointment of such inferior Officers, as they think proper, in the President alone, in the Courts of Law, or in the Heads of Departments.

(3) The President shall have Power to fill up all Vacancies that may happen during the Recess of the Senate, by granting Commissions which shall expire at the End of their next Session.

(1) *The President shall be Commander in Chief*: Civilian control of the military is absolutely critical for any government based on popular sovereignty.

   *the principal Officer in each of the executive Departments*: Although the Constitution says nothing about a president's "cabinet," we see here that the framers envisioned a multidepartment executive branch, each with a single head.

   *grant Reprieves and Pardons*: Why should a president be able to negate or preempt the judiciary? Alexander Hamilton offered one rationale: during an insurrection, pardoning some participants—a divide and conquer strategy—can be a useful tool for suppression. In practice, presidential pardons (most often in the last days of office) have appeared more discretionary than strategic.

(2) *He shall have Power, by and with the Advice and Consent of the Senate, to make Treaties*: *Consent* can be defined, but how, exactly, is a president to seek senatorial *Advice*? Early in his first term, George Washington entered the Senate chamber seeking *Advice and Consent* for a treaty with Creek Indians. Rather than give their hasty consent, senators discussed the matter and then sent it to committee, tabling it for a couple of days. George Washington had wanted a dialogue but didn't get one. "This defeats every purpose of my coming here," he reportedly said. One senator, William Maclay, complained that senators did not want "these advises and consents ravished, in a degree, from us." Whether a president must take the Senate's advice seriously remains as muddled today as it was at the start.

*provided two thirds of the Senators present concur*: The framers thought that the Senate, which provided the greatest continuity, should be truly onboard for any treaty—hence the need for a supermajority. Even so, only a president can *initiate* a treaty, and this worried James Madison. Might a president "derive so much power and importance from a state of war that he might be tempted, if authorized, to impede a treaty of peace?" (Consider Lyndon Johnson's Vietnam War and George W. Bush's Iraq War.) To prevent this, Madison suggested that the Senate could "make treaties of peace, without the concurrence of the President." This idea was defeated, however, so treaty-making power lies with the president.

Further, by law today, the president can make a "congressional-executive agreement," which requires only a simple majority of both the House and the Senate, or a "sole executive agreement," which does not require any consent. In 1998, the Made in the USA Foundation challenged the North American Free Trade Agreement (NAFTA), claiming the deal was a treaty and required ratification by two-thirds of the Senate. But a federal court held that Congress and the president have the constitutional authority to treat trade agreements as normal legislation—a "congressional-executive agreement"—and that ruling still stands. But if a president wants to *withdraw* from a such an agreement, must Congress approve the action? This constitutional issue

echoes one that was hotly debated, and nar-
rowly decided, by the First Federal Congress—
see immediately below.

*with the Advice and Consent of the
Senate . . . appoint Ambassadors, other public
Ministers and Consuls, Judges of the supreme
Court*: Here, *Consent* presents an interpre-
tive problem. In 1789, Congress created a
Department of Foreign Affairs, to be headed
by a secretary who would be "removable
from office by the President of the United
States." Some congressmen challenged that:
If the president required senatorial consent
for an *appointment,* shouldn't consent also
be required for *removal*? That seems logical,
but the Constitution never states this in so
many words.

James Madison thought Senate consent
for removal was a terrible idea. A secretary of
foreign affairs could endure in office indefinitely by courting the approval of senators;
presidents, by contrast, might come and go
every four years. Department chiefs would
rule over their respective fiefdoms, while "the
power of the President"—supposedly the chief
executive—would be reduced "to a mere
vapor."

With the Constitution silent, the First Federal Congress was left to decide. Only because

Vice President John Adams broke a tie in the Senate was the matter finally settled in favor of the president's exclusive removal power.

*Consent of the Senate* is still a contentious issue. That body has the authority to withhold consent from an individual nominee, but can it refuse even to *consider* a nominee? In 2016, by announcing it would take no action on any of President Obama's nominees to the Supreme Court, the Senate issued a *blanket* denial of consent. The following year, angry Democrats countered by filibustering the approval of President Trump's nominee for the open seat, Neil Gorsuch, but Republicans suspended the three-fifths requirement for cloture and confirmed the nomination. (See discussion for Article I, Section 5, Clause 2.) The framers did not foresee the political manipulation of this clause.

(3) *The President shall have Power to fill up all Vacancies that may happen during the Recess of the Senate*: This is another efficiency-driven provision. The framers did not expect the Senate to be in session year-round, but the president would remain on duty. Why wait for months to fill a judgeship or a key executive position?

Historically, presidents have made recess

appointments when the Senate has failed to act on their nominees. The Senate can prevent that, however, by holding "pro forma" sessions. (See the discussion for Article I, Section 5, Clause 4.) In actuality, the Senate might recess, but formally it is still in session.

## SECTION. 3.

He shall from time to time give to the Congress Information of the State of the Union, and recommend to their Consideration such Measures as he shall judge necessary and expedient; he may, on extraordinary Occasions, convene both Houses, or either of them, and in Case of Disagreement between them, with Respect to the Time of Adjournment, he may adjourn them to such Time as he shall think proper; he shall receive Ambassadors and other public Ministers; he shall take Care that the Laws be faithfully executed, and shall Commission all the Officers of the United States.

*give to the Congress Information of the State of the Union, and recommend to their Consideration such Measures*: A president's State of the Union address is part of the job description. From the outset, *Information* has included a president's recommendations—

but these have no force unless or until Congress acts.

*in Case of Disagreement ... he may adjourn them to such Time as he shall think proper*: Yet another efficiency measure. One house of Congress cannot avoid the other simply by adjourning.

*receive Ambassadors and other public Ministers*: Someone must represent the nation, and that is the president. This provision is often cited to support the president's primacy in developing foreign policy.

*he shall take Care that the Laws be faithfully executed*: Note the word *faithfully*. A president is not only authorized but also obligated to execute the laws, even if he or she does not agree with some of their provisions. Executive orders are based on this clause, but there are limits. An executive order must implement either an act of Congress or a provision of the Constitution.

When Congress drafts legislation, it often assigns its implementation to a particular executive agency. The Environmental Protection Agency, for example, is charged with carrying out more than two dozen acts—not only the Clean Air Act, Clean Water Act, and Endangered Species Act but also the Oil Pollution Act, Toxic Substances Control

Act, and Nuclear Waste Policy Act. Officials of the EPA must, by law, implement each of these acts. A president appoints the administrator of the EPA, but once appointed, that person is responsible to Congress as well as to the president and must *faithfully* follow the letter and the spirit of all enabling legislation.

### SECTION. 4.

**The President, Vice President and all civil Officers of the United States, shall be removed from Office on Impeachment for, and Conviction of, Treason, Bribery, or other high Crimes and Misdemeanors.**

There are three impeachable infractions, two specific and one open-ended. The framers signaled a direction, but it is not a precise map. *Other high Crimes and Misdemeanors* leaves ample room for interpretation.

## ARTICLE. III.

### SECTION. 1.

**The judicial Power of the United States, shall be vested in one supreme Court, and in such inferior Courts as the Congress**

may from time to time ordain and establish. The Judges, both of the supreme and inferior Courts, shall hold their Offices during good Behaviour, and shall, at stated Times, receive for their Services, a Compensation, which shall not be diminished during their Continuance in Office.

*one supreme Court, and in such inferior Courts as the Congress may from time to time ordain and establish*: The Constitution is minimalist here. It establishes only one court, leaving Congress to build the remainder of the judicial edifice. It does not say how many justices must serve on the Supreme Court, nor does it specify any qualification for the office. Hamilton, in Federalist No. 78, called the federal judiciary the "weakest of the three departments of power" and the "least dangerous to the political rights of the Constitution." Many today would argue that point, but it was certainly the least developed by the framers.

*Judges . . . shall hold their Offices during good Behaviour*: This means for life or until voluntary retirement, unless a judge is impeached. According to Article II, Section 2, Clause 2, Supreme Court justices are appointed by the president with the advice and consent of the Senate, and Congress has extended this to include all federal judges.

Why aren't federal judges elected, and why do they serve for life? In colonial times, royal governors influenced judges. That would never do, nor did the framers want judges to come under popular pressure when making their decisions. Lifelong appointments ensured independence. "Unelected judges"—a loud complaint today—was fundamental to the framers' plan for an impartial judiciary.

### SECTION. 2.

**(1) The judicial Power shall extend to all Cases, in Law and Equity, arising under this Constitution, the Laws of the United States, and Treaties made, or which shall be made, under their Authority;—to all Cases affecting Ambassadors, other public Ministers and Consuls;—to all Cases of admiralty and maritime Jurisdiction;—to Controversies to which the United States shall be a Party;—to Controversies between two or more States;—~~between a State and Citizens of another State,~~—between Citizens of different States,—between Citizens of the same State claiming Lands under Grants of different States, and between**

a State, or the Citizens thereof, and foreign States, Citizens or Subjects.

(2) In all Cases affecting Ambassadors,
other public Ministers and Consuls, and
those in which a State shall be Party, the
supreme Court shall have original Jurisdiction. In all the other Cases before
mentioned, the supreme Court shall have
appellate Jurisdiction, both as to Law and
Fact, with such Exceptions, and under such
Regulations as the Congress shall make.

(3) The Trial of all Crimes, except in Cases
of Impeachment, shall be by Jury; and such
Trial shall be held in the State where the
said Crimes shall have been committed;
but when not committed within any State,
the Trial shall be at such Place or Places
as the Congress may by Law have directed.

(1) *The judicial Power shall extend to all
Cases, in Law and Equity, arising under this
Constitution, the Laws of the United States,
and Treaties*: Federal judges adjudicate federal law.

*to all Cases affecting Ambassadors, other
public Ministers and Consuls;—to all Cases of
admiralty and maritime Jurisdiction*: In short,

all cases with international implications or involving federal officials.

—*to Controversies*: Federal judges are referees when *Controversies* cross state and international lines.

*between a State and Citizens of another State*: This was superseded by the Eleventh Amendment.

(2) *original Jurisdiction* versus *appellate Jurisdiction*: For the most part, the Supreme Court hears only appeals. The list for "original Jurisdiction," although short, presents something of a problem: What happens when one state sues another for dumping its sewage across the state line? With no lower court to conduct a trial, the Supreme Court must start from scratch and determine matters of fact. Theoretically, the court would conduct its own trial, but that would be far too time-consuming. Instead, it appoints so-called special masters to do the work that lower courts generally do, a work-around the framers did not envision.

(3) *The Trial of all Crimes . . . shall be by Jury*: Trial by jury dates back at least as far as the Magna Carta. The framers neglected to con-

sider some finer points of criminal justice that would be addressed in the Bill of Rights, but they could not possibly exclude this most fundamental right. Note that this clause covers only criminal trials. The Seventh Amendment guarantees the right to a jury trial in most civil cases.

*and such Trial shall be held in the State where the said Crimes shall have been committed*: In colonial times, some trials were held in faraway places, a practice that was not only inconvenient but also prejudicial to the outcomes.

## SECTION. 3.

**(1) Treason against the United States, shall consist only in levying War against them, or in adhering to their Enemies, giving them Aid and Comfort. No Person shall be convicted of Treason unless on the Testimony of two Witnesses to the same overt Act, or on Confession in open Court.**

**(2) The Congress shall have Power to declare the Punishment of Treason, but no Attainder of Treason shall work Corruption of Blood, or Forfeiture except during the Life of the Person attainted.**

(1) *Treason against the United States, shall consist only in levying War against them, or in adhering to their Enemies, giving them Aid and Comfort*: The framers debated the definition of treason at some length. By being precise, they hoped to prevent casual accusations of treason from being used as political weapons. During times of national stress, however, accusations of giving *Aid and Comfort* to an enemy have been tossed about rather freely.

*the same overt Act*: Talk is cheap, not in itself an *overt Act*. If talking trash about the government were treasonous, many thousands or millions could be declared traitors today.

(2) *Corruption of Blood, or Forfeiture except during the Life of the Person attainted*: *Corruption of Blood* sounds gruesome, but this clause has a benign purpose: punishment for treason should not deprive a traitor's heirs of their inheritance. We do not worry about this today; that the framers *did* worry about it signals how different their world was from ours.

So ends Article III without a mention of judicial review. The Constitution does not give the Supreme Court the *explicit* authority to declare laws unconstitutional, but does the court have an *implicit* authority? How has judicial review become such an integral part of our governing process?

At the Constitutional Convention, several (but certainly not all) delegates assumed that judges would have the power of "judicial nullification," as they said at the time. A judge's "exposition of the laws," said Elbridge Gerry, necessarily involves "a power of deciding on their Constitutionality." "As to the Constitutionality of laws," Luther Martin observed, "judges . . . have a negative." James Madison thought that the Constitution would sometimes "oblige" judges to declare a law "null & void." Why, then, didn't the framers write this into the Constitution?

Imagine how that would have played with the public: unelected judges overturning the will of the people, expressed through acts of an elected legislature. This would have sounded no better then than it does now, and it might well have jeopardized ratification.

But if judges can't declare a law unconstitutional, who can? Opinions differed at the time. Some said the president could make sure his own acts were constitutional, and Congress could judge its own acts as well.

But what if those two branches differed over who, for instance, has the constitutional power to shape foreign policy? (In fact, that was hotly contested in the 1790s.) Who should settle such a dispute?

Some at the time said "the people themselves" should decide—scholars today call this "popular constitutionalism." But how are the people, in aggregate, to make that decision, and how can they implement it?

Slowly, on its own, the Supreme Court asserted its authority to determine constitutionality. In *Hylton v. United* States (1796), it ruled that a law *was* constitutional, but by so doing, it implied that it might have ruled the other way. Then in *Marbury v. Madison* (1803), it declared a law to be unconstitutional. No other law was ruled unconstitutional until 1857, when the infamous Dred Scott decision dictated that escaped slaves must be returned to their masters. Since then, however, Americans have come to accept, often begrudgingly, that the high court has the last word. In *Bush v. Gore* (2000), it effectively determined the outcome of a contested presidential election—and the losers saw no choice but to abide.

Even so, we continue to complain about "activist judges"—when things don't go our way, that is. If you are a staunch supporter of the right to bear arms and your town decides to *permit* the carrying of guns in public, you don't want some activist judge to interfere. On the other hand, you *will* want the courts to interfere if your town *outlaws* the carrying of guns in public, which, in your opinion, violates the Second Amendment. Competing and often malleable interpretations of the Constitution provide a playing field for our continuing debates.

## ARTICLE. IV.

### SECTION. 1.

**Full Faith and Credit shall be given in each State to the public Acts, Records, and judicial Proceedings of every other State. And the Congress may by general Laws prescribe the Manner in which such Acts, Records and Proceedings shall be proved, and the Effect thereof.**

Before *Obergefell v. Hodges* (2015), which ruled that same-sex marriage is legal through-out the nation, advocates of same-sex mar-riage pointed to the first sentence: a same-sex marriage in one state should be given *Full*

*Faith and Credit* in *every other State.* But in 1996, Congress used the second sentence to support its Defense of Marriage Act, which defined marriage as a union between a man and a woman. The framers never imagined this legal tangle.

### SECTION. 2.

**(1) The Citizens of each State shall be entitled to all Privileges and Immunities of Citizens in the several States.**

**(2) A Person charged in any State with Treason, Felony, or other Crime, who shall flee from Justice, and be found in another State, shall on Demand of the executive Authority of the State from which he fled, be delivered up, to be removed to the State having Jurisdiction of the Crime.**

**(3)** ~~No Person held to Service or Labour in one State, under the Laws thereof, escaping into another, shall, in Consequence of any Law or Regulation therein, be discharged from such Service or Labour, but shall be delivered up on Claim of the Party to whom such Service or Labour may be due.~~

(1) *entitled to all Privileges and Immunities of Citizens in the several States*: Some compare this clause to Article I, Section 8, Clause 3, the interstate commerce clause, which also breaks down interstate barriers. Opinions differ on how to apply it, however. The confusion is understandable, considering the broad phraseology of *Privileges and Immunities*. Note that Section 1 of the Fourteenth Amendment echoes this wording, substituting *citizens of the United States* for *Citizens in the several States*.

(2) *A Person charged in any State with Treason, Felony, or other Crime, who shall flee from Justice, and be found in another State, shall . . . be removed to the State having Jurisdiction of the Crime*: This clause mandates extradition and interstate law enforcement cooperation.

(3) *Person held to Service or Labour in one State, under the Laws thereof, escaping into another*: Shorthand for escaped slaves.
   *shall be delivered up on Claim of the Party to whom such Service or Labour may be due*: The so-called fugitive slave clause, part of the compromise over slave importation (See Arti-

cle I, Section 9, Clause 1), was superseded by the Thirteenth Amendment's ban on "slavery" and "involuntary servitude."

### SECTION. 3.

**(1) New States may be admitted by the Congress into this Union; but no new State shall be formed or erected within the Jurisdiction of any other State; nor any State be formed by the Junction of two or more States, or Parts of States, without the Consent of the Legislatures of the States concerned as well as of the Congress.**

**(2) The Congress shall have Power to dispose of and make all needful Rules and Regulations respecting the Territory or other Property belonging to the United States; and nothing in this Constitution shall be so construed as to Prejudice any Claims of the United States, or of any particular State.**

(1) *New States may be admitted by the Congress into this Union*: This clause grants to Congress a power already exercised under the Articles of Confederation. As the framers deliberated in Philadelphia, the Continental

Congress, meeting in New York whenever it could muster a quorum, passed the Northwest Ordinance, which spelled out how new states could enter the Union. (In 1789, the First Federal Congress incorporated the Northwest Ordinance with only minor revisions.)

*no new State shall be formed or erected within the Jurisdiction of any other State; nor any State be formed by the Junction of two or more States, or Parts of States, without the Consent of the Legislatures of the States concerned as well as of the Congress:* Secession from a state or states is no easy task—Congress and the state legislature(s) must be onboard. Vermont left New York, but that was essentially a fait accompli at the time of the Convention. When West Virginia seceded from Virginia during the Civil War, it didn't need Virginia's approval because Virginia had itself seceded from the Union. There have been other attempts, but only these two have succeeded.

(2) *Congress shall have Power to dispose of and make all needful Rules and Regulations respecting the Territory or other Property belonging to the United States:* This gave Congress the authority to ban slavery in the territories, but it also gives our current

Congress the authority to sell off National Parks if it chooses to do so. Vigilant citizens, beware!

### SECTION. 4.

**The United States shall guarantee to every State in this Union a Republican Form of Government, and shall protect each of them against Invasion; and on Application of the Legislature, or of the Executive (when the Legislature cannot be convened), against domestic Violence.**

This is a curious provision, the only *obligation* placed on the federal government as a whole. What were the framers worried about here?

The *Invasion* part is easy. Without this obligation, if Canada invades along our shared border, Congress and the commander in chief might deem it strategically advantageous to concede North Dakota without a fight—sorry, North Dakotans. In 1787, with Spain posing a threat on the west and Britain on the north, such a scenario was not out of the question.

The rest is more complicated. The framers worried that *domestic Violence,* such as Massachusetts had recently experienced, might result in mob rule and the overthrow of a state's *Republican Form of Government.* ("Republican," of course, signifies a government run by the people's chosen representatives, not a political party.) Nathaniel Gorham, from Massachusetts, imagined where that chaos might end: "An enterprising Citizen might erect the standard of Monarchy in a particular State, might gather together partizans from all quarters, might extend his views from State to State, and threaten to establish a tyranny over the whole & the Genl. Govt. be compelled to remain an inactive witness of its own destruction." This is not as far-fetched as it sounds—consider the rise of fascism in post–World War I Europe, fueled by social and economic mayhem. Consider also Gouverneur Morris's prescient remark at the Constitutional Convention: "The rich will take advantage of their [the people's] passions & make these the instruments for oppressing them. . . . They always did. They always will." To guard against threats from the mindless many, the ambitious few, or both, the framers insisted that the federal government make a stand at the state level, where they thought such threats would most likely originate.

But only if asked, of course—*on Applica-*

*tion of the Legislature.* Elbridge Gerry, also of Massachusetts, opposed "letting loose the myrmidons of the U. States on a State without its own consent."

## ARTICLE. V.

The Congress, whenever two thirds of both Houses shall deem it necessary, shall propose Amendments to this Constitution, or, on the Application of the Legislatures of two thirds of the several States, shall call a Convention for proposing Amendments, which, in either Case, shall be valid to all Intents and Purposes, as Part of this Constitution, when ratified by the Legislatures of three fourths of the several States, or by Conventions in three fourths thereof, as the one or the other Mode of Ratification may be proposed by the Congress; Provided that no Amendment which may be made prior to the Year One thousand eight hundred and eight shall in any Manner affect the first and fourth Clauses in the Ninth Section of the first Article; and that no State, without its Consent, shall be deprived of its equal Suffrage in the Senate.

We treat the framers as all-knowing, but they fully acknowledged that the plan they created was forged by compromise and far from perfect. With time, there would have to be adjustments. The Articles of Confederation had failed to provide a workable system for change; their new Constitution, by contrast, would provide alternate paths for amendments, should one path or the other prove inadequate.

Either two-thirds of both the Senate and House of Representatives can propose an amendment, or two-thirds of the state legislatures can call a national convention for the purpose of proposing one or more amendments. Fearing that either Congress or state legislatures might resist change, the framers allowed *either* group to initiate the process.

The framers also allowed for alternative methods of approval. If Congress suspects that state legislatures will oppose needed changes, it can appeal to the people through state conventions.

Although the need for unanimous approval had proved unworkable, the framers created a high hurdle for ratification. Elsewhere, when they required a supermajority, they placed the threshold at two-thirds, or 67 percent. (That was the number for the Senate's ratification of a treaty, a congressional override of a presidential veto, and to initiate the amendment process.) But to alter the fundamental structure of the government, they demanded ratification by three-quarters (75 percent) of the states.

Today, if Congress does not propose an amendment, thirty-four of the fifty states must agree to call a national convention, and then thirty-eight of the fifty states must ratify any amendment that the convention proposes. In a sharply bifurcated political environment, these hurdles are extremely difficult to clear. If an amendment is perceived as giving either side even the slightest advantage, the other side will be able to kill it.

Difficult but not impossible. Twenty-eight states have called for a national convention to consider an amendment requiring a balanced federal budget every year. Republicans, who generally support the measure, currently control thirty-one state assemblies and are within reach of the thirty-four states needed to call a convention. But then the extreme supermajority kicks in. With thirty-eight states required for ratification, it would take only thirteen states to defeat the amendment.

Meanwhile, progressive Democrats are pushing for amendments that would overturn the Supreme Court's decision in *Citizens*

*United v. FEC* (2010), which threw out limits
on campaign finance, and even further, deny
corporations the rights of people, which, by
a hotly contested interpretation of the Fourteenth Amendment (see below), corporations
currently enjoy. This movement, because it
proposes to limit the influence of money in
politics, will face a greater obstacle yet: stiff
resistance from moneyed interests that currently do influence politics.

## ARTICLE. VI.

(1) All Debts contracted and Engagements
entered into, before the Adoption of this
Constitution, shall be as valid against the
United States under this Constitution, as
under the Confederation.

(2) This Constitution, and the Laws of the
United States which shall be made in Pursuance thereof; and all Treaties made, or
which shall be made, under the Authority
of the United States, shall be the supreme
Law of the Land; and the Judges in every
State shall be bound thereby, any Thing
in the Constitution or Laws of any State to
the Contrary notwithstanding.

**(3) The Senators and Representatives before mentioned, and the Members of the several State Legislatures, and all executive and judicial Officers, both of the United States and of the several States, shall be bound by Oath or Affirmation, to support this Constitution; but no religious Test shall ever be required as a Qualification to any Office or public Trust under the United States.**

(1) *All Debts contracted . . . before the Adoption of this Constitution, shall be . . . valid against the United States*: Adopting a new Constitution was not to be construed as filing bankruptcy. To secure public credit, the framers, many of whom held government securities, pledged that the nation would make good on its debts.

(2) *This Constitution, and the Laws of the United States which shall be made in Pursuance thereof; and all Treaties made, . . . shall be the supreme Law of the Land*: This is key to it all. With great self-confidence, the Constitution declares its own supremacy.

Note that treaties are included as well as laws. In 1785, a proposed treaty with Britain, which traded away access to the Mississippi River for commercial favors that benefited

northeastern merchants, caused great controversy. The framers worried that Americans
who objected to an international treaty might
not abide by it. Under the Constitution, treaties enjoy equal force with laws.

*the Judges in every State shall be bound
thereby*: State judges are charged with adju-
dicating state laws, but they cannot disregard
federal law.

*any Thing in the Constitution or Laws of
any State to the Contrary notwithstanding*:
Here is a clear declaration of federal supremacy. Although difficult for some to swallow, it
is the very core of the Constitution.

(3) *shall be bound by Oath or Affirmation,
to support this Constitution*: Not only the
president but all federal and state officials,
elected or appointed, must pledge to oper-
ate in accordance with the Constitution. The
word *support* suggests that allegiance should
not be grudging.

*but no religious Test shall ever be required
as a Qualification to any Office or public
Trust*: This nod to freedom of religion preceded the addition of the First Amendment,
ensuring from the start that religious beliefs
have no bearing on qualifications for public
office.

## ARTICLE. VII.

**The Ratification of the Conventions of nine States, shall be sufficient for the Establishment of this Constitution between the States so ratifying the Same.**

The framers sent their proposed Constitution to state conventions rather than state legislatures for two reasons. Politically, state legislatures stood to lose some power by the new rules and would be more likely to turn them down. Philosophically, the framers thought that the Constitution would have greater force if the people elected representatives for the sole purpose of approving the government under which they would live.

Not all states were likely to favor the plan. Probably Rhode Island, and possibly other states, would object to a new and "energetic" federal government. The framers therefore decided that once a certain number of states had ratified, the new system would kick in—and then the holdouts would join rather than be left out. But how many did they need to start? A bare majority of seven would not be an impressive beginning. Eight, nine, and ten were proposed. There was no particular logic to choosing nine (69 percent of 13) instead of eight (62 percent) or ten (77 percent). Possibly, when the framers surveyed the political map, they thought nine was an achievable goal.

**done in Convention by the Unanimous Consent of the States present the Seventeenth Day of September in the Year of our Lord one thousand seven hundred and Eighty seven and of the Independance of the United States of America the Twelfth In witness whereof We have hereunto subscribed our Names,**

*G°. Washington*
*Presidt and deputy from Virginia*

DELAWARE
*Geo: Read*
*Gunning Bedford jun*
*John Dickinson*
*Richard Bassett*
*Jaco: Broom*

MARYLAND
*James McHenry*
*Dan of St Thos. Jenifer*
*Danl. Carroll*

### VIRGINIA
*John Blair*
*James Madison Jr.*

### NORTH CAROLINA
*Wm. Blount*
*Richd. Dobbs Spaight*
*Hu Williamson*

### SOUTH CAROLINA
*J. Rutledge*
*Charles Cotesworth Pinckney*
*Charles Pinckney*
*Pierce Butler*

### GEORGIA
*William Few*
*Abr Baldwin*

### NEW HAMPSHIRE
*John Langdon*
*Nicholas Gilman*

### MASSACHUSETTS
*Nathaniel Gorham*
*Rufus King*

### CONNECTICUT
*Wm. Saml. Johnson*
*Roger Sherman*

NEW YORK
*Alexander Hamilton*


NEW JERSEY
*Wil: Livingston*
*David Brearley*
*Wm. Paterson*
*Jona: Dayton*


PENSYLVANIA
*B Franklin*
*Thomas Mifflin*
*Robt. Morris*
*Geo. Clymer*
*Thos. FitzSimons*
*Jared Ingersoll*
*James Wilson*
*Gouv Morris*


*Unanimous Consent of the States present*:
As throughout the Convention, voting was
by state delegation. Rhode Island had never
participated, and New York, with only one
delegate remaining, could not cast a vote.
The other eleven delegations all approved the
final draft.

*and of the Independance of the United*
*States of America the Twelfth [Year]*: After
revolutions, some nations reboot their calen-

dars. We tried that, too, although it didn't stick. September 17, 1787, was within the twelfth year since the United States declared its independence.

To demonstrate their support, most delegates signed the document. Only three who were present at the conclusion of the Convention refused to sign: George Mason and Edmund Randolph of Virginia and Elbridge Gerry of Massachusetts. (Four delegates who wanted to improve the Articles of Confederation rather than create a strong central government—Maryland's Luther Martin and John Francis Mercer and New York's Robert Yates and John Lansing, Jr.—had left earlier.) Those who did not sign thought that popular discontent with the proposed plan would *produce* "anarchy" and "civil convulsions." Those who signed the Constitution believed that it would *prevent* anarchy and civil convulsions.

*Part Two*

# BILL OF RIGHTS

## BACKGROUND

Anglo-Americans have always embraced a culture of rights. The first colonial charter, granted to the founders of Virginia in 1606, promised that people who emigrated to America would "have and enjoy all liberties, franchises, and immunities . . . as if they had been abiding and born, within this our realm of England." In several other colonies, either the Crown or the colonial proprietors specified liberties that the government was duty bound to respect. In Maryland, Massachusetts, and New York, the people themselves, through their representatives in the legislatures, passed laws that foreshadowed the Bill of Rights.

The 1641 Massachusetts Body of Liberties listed ninety-eight specific rights. Number forty-five, for example, stated: "No man shall be forced by Torture to confesse any Crime

against himselfe nor any other unlesse it be
in some Capitall case where he is first fullie
convicted by cleare and suffitient evidence
to be guilty." Protections for those accused
of crimes included a right to post bail, legal
representation, presentation of evidence, a
speedy trial by jury, appeal to a higher court,
and security against double jeopardy, along
with a prohibition against "bodilie punishments" that are "inhumane Barbarous or
cruel." (This meant no more than forty lashes,
"unles his crime be very shamefull.")

The guarantees of the Massachusetts Body
of Liberties did not end there. Foreigners
escaping persecution were to be welcomed.
Monopolies were prohibited. No man could
be pressed into fighting an offensive war
without his consent. Parents could not "wil-
fullie and unreasonably deny any childe timely
or convenient mariage." Servants could flee
from cruel masters, and if a master "smite
out" an eye or a tooth, the servant could go
free. Witches, on the other hand, were to be
put to death, as were blasphemers, adulter-
ers, and homosexuals. The secured rights are
all the more striking because they were protected by a puritanical society we know more
for its witch hunts than for its attention to
personal liberties.

With independence in 1776, all eleven states that drafted new constitutions detailed many rights. Seven opened with lists reminiscent of the Massachusetts Body of Liberties from the preceding century. All these affirmed that government must be rooted in the people and that people could only be taxed by their own representatives. They also guaranteed, in one form or another, freedom of the press, freedom of worship, and various rights for people accused of crimes. A few included features we do not generally associate with those times: proportional taxation, whereby each citizen would be taxed according to his ability to pay, and a prohibition against monopolies.

Strangely enough, the framers of the Constitution did not follow the precedent set by colonial charters and state constitutions. Almost as an afterthought, five days before the Convention would adjourn, George Mason proposed the addition of a bill of rights, but the weary framers rejected his idea without even discussing it. Two weeks later, before the Continental Congress forwarded the proposed new Constitution to the states for ratification, Richard Henry Lee moved that Congress append a bill of rights—but that, too, was summarily dismissed.

The framers' neglect was a colossal political blunder. They failed to realize that an express declaration of rights would make their plan more palatable to Americans who had come to expect such assurances. In the debates over ratification, the absence of a bill of rights became a major rallying cry for those who opposed ratification.

Several state ratification conventions suggested amendments to the Constitution. Many of these secured rights that had been guaranteed by colonial charters and state constitutions, but others addressed a wide range of concerns. New York's proposed amendments, for instance, included such pro-democracy measures as a larger House of Representatives, prohibition of government-sanctioned monopolies, term limits for senators and the president, restrictions on a standing army, a method for recalling senators, open meetings of Congress, and frequent publication of congressional proceedings, as well as returning authority over debtor relief to the states. One amendment, appearing on all the lists, toyed with the very cornerstone of the Constitution, federal taxation. Congress would first have to ask state legislatures for funds, and only if the legislatures failed to pay could it levy taxes.

Supporters of the proposed Constitution, calling themselves Federalists, feared that these sorts of amendments might unravel the elaborate web the framers had woven at the Convention. Amendments that merely protected rights, on the other hand, would really do no harm. If these were added pre-emptively, opponents of the proposed new plan might drop more invasive demands, and the essence of the Constitution would remain intact.

That was James Madison's strategy when he introduced amendments in the First Federal Congress. With his proposals, "the structure & stamina of the government are as little touched as possible," he asserted. Somewhat reluctantly, the Federalist-dominated Congress debated and revised Madison's list for several weeks. In the end, it recommended twelve amendments, ten of which were ratified by a sufficient number of states in 1791. To the framers we owe our governmental structure and the political rights embedded within it, but to other Americans, and to the clamor they created, we owe our Bill of Rights.

Ironically, Americans today celebrate the Constitution's add-ons more than the central document itself. Ask someone what they love most about the Constitution, and most likely they will highlight provisions within the Bill of Rights.

## AMENDMENT I (RATIFIED IN 1791)

**Congress shall make no law respecting an establishment of religion, or prohibiting the free exercise thereof; or abridging the freedom of speech, or of the press; or the right of the people peaceably to assemble, and to petition the Government for a redress of grievances.**

No politically conscious American is a stranger to the First Amendment. It permeates our civic culture and provides a language in which we argue many heated issues. Contrary to popular myth, however, First Amendment rights did not come first because they were deemed the most important. The first amendment on Congress's list was a complex regulation of the size of the House of Representatives. Never ratified, that one lost its place in line.

*Congress shall make no law*: Of the Bill of Rights amendments, this alone explicitly prohibits governmental action and has the force of law; the rest are positive declarations of

rights or principles, which, only by implication, the government must not violate. Note
that only the *federal* legislative body is
mentioned. Originally, states were restricted
not by the First Amendment but by declarations of rights within their own constitutions.
That has since changed, however. Starting in
the early twentieth century, applying a doctrine known as "incorporation," the Supreme
Court has held that most rights listed in the
first ten amendments apply to states as well.
According to Section 1 of the Fourteenth
Amendment (see below), no *State* can *deprive
any person of life, liberty, or property, without due process of law,* and one by one,
rights listed in the first ten amendments have
been included under that broad umbrella.

*no law respecting an establishment of reli-
gion* (the Establishment Clause): Government-
established religions can be very oppressive,
which is precisely why many Americans
emigrated from Europe and why this clause
prohibits the establishment of a *national* religion. (Not until *Everson v. Board of Education*
in 1947 was the establishment clause applied
to states.) But does this imply that the government needs to stay clear of any religious
organization or activity? School prayer, public vouchers for religious education, the so-

called War on Christmas—debates rage on, in and out of court.

In January 2017, when President Trump issued an executive order banning entry into the United States from seven predominantly Muslim nations, he vowed to exempt persecuted Christians and let them in. Many viewed this as a direct violation of the Establishment Clause. Weeks later, when the president issued a revised executive order, he omitted the commitment to favor Christians.

*or prohibiting the free exercise thereof* (the Free Exercise Clause): Few Americans object to "freedom of conscience," as the Founding Generation often called it, but issues arise when religious beliefs lead to *exercise* that others deem objectionable. Polygamy? Animal sacrifice? Where do we draw the line? Certainly, acts of terrorism committed in the name of a given religion cross that line, yet how do we punish criminals and safeguard citizens without religious profiling? The First Amendment protects the innocent from being targeted with the guilty.

*or abridging the freedom of speech, or of the press*: Both are indispensable to a free society, yet no freedom is absolute. The classic: "You can't cry 'fire' in a crowded theater." Other cases are not so clear-cut. Does preaching violence lead to violent actions? What counts as "hate speech," and should it be protected? We struggle to define the limits.

Now, there is a twist the Founding Generation did not envision: Can money be counted as speech? The Supreme Court, in *Citizens United,* has said yes, but many think that treating money as speech, with no effective limits, allows the few to control the many, not what the First Federal Congress intended nor what we prefer.

*or the right of the people peaceably to assemble, and to petition the Government for a redress of grievances*: These are rights that the people, collectively, must have if they are to have any say in their government. But how *much* say should people have in their government? The First Federal Congress, when preparing its list of amendments, devoted more time to this subject than to any other. At issue was whether the United States should be a *republic*—a representative government in which elected leaders are free to deliberate and decide on their own—or a *democracy,* in which representatives follow the lead of their constituents.

Virginia's ratifying convention, which Madison used as a model for his proposals, had

included the words "or to instruct their representatives" between the right to assemble
and the right to petition. Some congressmen tried to put that back in. One argued:
"Under a democracy, whose great end is to
form a code of laws congenial with the public sentiment, the popular opinion ought to
be collected and attended to. Our Government is derived from the people, of consequence the people have a right to consult
for the common good." A congressman on
the other side responded: "Representation
is the principle of our Government; the people ought to have confidence in the honor
and integrity of those they send forward
to transact their business." Back and forth
they went, and in the end they decided by a
vote of 41 to 10 *not* to include the right of
the people to instruct their representatives.
The United States would be a republic, not
a democracy.

In time, democracy would make a stron-
ger showing, and some of this has been written into the Constitution. The right to vote
is broadened by the Fifteenth, Seventeenth,
Nineteenth, Twenty-Third, Twenty-Fourth, and
Twenty-Sixth Amendments. In practice, people today expect those whom they elect to
respond to their wants. Today, a congress-

man who proclaims that "the people ought to have confidence in the honor and integrity of those they send forward to transact their business" will have to answer for that remark at the ballot box. We don't instruct our representatives formally, but we behave as if we have that right.

## AMENDMENT II (RATIFIED IN 1791)

**A well regulated Militia, being necessary to the security of a free State, the right of the people to keep and bear Arms, shall not be infringed.**

Separating the two components in this amendment is the most disputed comma in history. For gun-safety advocates, the comma links the dependent and independent clauses of the sentence, the first providing the reason for the second. The whole amendment refers to militias, they maintain. Gun-rights advocates note that commas at the time were not used as they are today. They argue that the amendment makes two distinct statements, the first about militias and the second about (private) gun ownership.

Each side marshals evidence to support

its position. Gun-safety advocates point to records of the First Federal Congress, where the amendment was hammered out. Debates there focused on two issues. First, should religious pacifists be exempt from militia service? And second, might the federal government, which under the new Constitution had control of state militias, come to rely on a standing army and allow militias to lapse? This amendment ensured the preservation of a *well regulated Militia.* ("Well regulated" meant trained, disciplined, and fully functional.) There was no discussion at all about private ownership of guns.

They also point to several state constitutions in effect at the time that declared the people's right to keep and bear arms for a public purpose: "for the common defence" (Massachusetts), "for the safe defence of a free government" (Delaware), or "for the defence of the State" (North Carolina). Amendments proposed by state ratifying conventions favored militias as alternatives to a standing army. From the Virginia Convention:

"That the people have a right to keep and bear arms; that a well regulated Militia composed of the body of the people trained to arms is the proper, natural and safe defence of a free State. That standing armies in time of peace are dangerous to liberty, and therefore ought to be avoided, as far as the circumstances and protection of the Community will admit; and that in all cases the military should be under strict subordination to and governed by the Civil power."

Gun-rights advocates point to an amendment proposed by New Hampshire's ratifying convention: "Congress shall never disarm any Citizen unless such as are or have been in Actual Rebellion." Their strongest evidence for private use is a minority report that was never adopted from Pennsylvania's ratifying convention:

"That the people have a right to bear arms for the defence of themselves and their own State, or the United States, or for the purpose of killing game; and no law shall be passed for disarming the people or any of them, unless for crimes committed, or real danger of public injury from individuals; and as standing armies in time of peace are dangerous to liberty, they ought not to be kept up; and that the military shall be kept under strict subordination to and be governed by the civil power."

In truth, the lively debate over private ownership of guns is our own doing. Founding Era Americans supported gun rights *and* gun safety—they saw no conflict between the two. Of course citizens had the right to have muskets, for their own use as well as for militia service. (Even if the Second Amendment concerned only militia, that might be because private gun ownership was so accepted that it was rarely questioned.) But safety was a concern as well. The danger to public safety at that time came from gunpowder, which could explode and cause fires if not stored properly. Cities and towns placed limits on how much could be kept in private houses, and those limits were taken seriously.

When the First Federal Congress composed the Second Amendment, and when states ratified it, nobody imagined that a single individual could possess an automatic weapon capable of killing dozens of people in a matter of seconds. How would congressmen then have addressed this, had they anticipated it? We can only conjecture. Gun rights and gun safety: this is a legitimate issue for *our* time but one that the Constitution does not resolve.

## AMENDMENT III (RATIFIED IN 1791)

No Soldier shall, in time of peace be quartered in any house, without the consent of the Owner, nor in time of war, but in a manner to be prescribed by law.

The presence of British soldiers in Revolutionary times continued to rankle. The Constitution authorizes Congress to "raise and support" a standing army, but soldiers should not run roughshod over civilian populations. Today, the Third Amendment appears archaic, but it certainly made sense back then.

## AMENDMENT IV (RATIFIED IN 1791)

The right of the people to be secure in their persons, houses, papers, and effects, against unreasonable searches and seizures, shall not be violated, and no Warrants shall issue, but upon probable cause, supported by Oath or affirmation, and particularly describing the place to be searched, and the persons or things to be seized.

Merchant smugglers, hoping to evade import duties, were the first American patriots. In the early 1760s, they complained loudly about "writs of assistance"—blanket search warrants, of indefinite duration, that gave customs officials the authority to search ships or storehouses or homes at will. Writs of assistance were blunt instruments for law enforcement; the Fourth Amendment turns warrants into surgical scalpels. Officials must know what they are looking for and show good reasons for why they might find it in a particular place or in the possession of a specific person or persons.

What if a search that does not conform to these standards turns up incriminating evidence? Since 1914 for federal cases, and 1961 for state cases, such evidence has not been permitted in court. As with restrictions required by the Fifth and Sixth Amendments, enforcement officers might find this a nuisance, but that is precisely the point. Law and order works for the citizenry only if the laws themselves, and those enforcing them, are orderly.

## AMENDMENT V (RATIFIED IN 1791)

No person shall be held to answer for a capital, or otherwise infamous crime, unless on a presentment or indictment of a Grand Jury, except in cases arising in the land or naval forces, or in the Militia, when in actual service in time of War or public danger; nor shall any person be subject for the same offence to be twice put in jeopardy of life or limb; nor shall be compelled in any criminal case to be a witness against himself, nor be deprived of life, liberty, or property, without due process of law; nor shall private property be taken for public use, without just compensation.

This is a dizzying list of rights of the accused. Let's take them one by one:

*presentment or indictment of a Grand Jury*: In colonial times, grand juries shielded citizens from political prosecutions by Crown officials. Boston grand juries in the 1760s refused to indict leaders of the Stamp Act protests and newspaper editors accused of libeling the royal governor. Grand juries also weighed in on pressing issues. In 1776, six weeks before the Continental Congress declared independence, a grand jury presentment in the Cheraws District of South Carolina concluded that "the King and Parliament of Great Britain," by evidencing "every mark of cruelty and oppression," had "reduced this Colony to a state of separation from her," and that separation, although forced, was "the only lasting means of future happiness and safety." Because grand jurors are selected from the citizenry and make decisions directly, not through elected representatives, they are inherently democratic—if they are chosen from a broad range of the citizenry, that is.

*for the same offence . . . twice put in jeopardy of life or limb*: For the accused, a trial is punishment in itself. Imagine if double jeopardy, or multiple jeopardy, were permitted. Prosecutors could conduct one trial to feel things out, see what emerges, and then use that evidence to go at the accused again. This restriction ensures that prosecutors give it their best shot from the start, and if they fail, the accused goes free.

*nor shall be compelled . . . to be a witness against himself*: "Taking the fifth," though often viewed by the public as an implicit admission of guilt, is the Constitution's anti-torture provision—the methods by which the accused could be *compelled,* historically, knew no bounds.

*nor be deprived of life, liberty, or property, without due process of law*: Little wonder this clause is so often cited in court: the right to *life, liberty, or property* covers the gamut, and *due process* includes everything the Constitution states elsewhere about criminal proceedings. But does due process refer only to the sum total of constitutionally mandated *procedures,* or might it have a meaning, or *substance,* of its own? Are there restrictions not delineated, or rights not specifically guaranteed (see the Ninth Amendment), that are inherently part of our civic culture and therefore part of the "due process of law" Americans have come to expect? "Procedural due process" versus "substantive due process"—welcome to the world of constitutional litigation.

*nor shall private property be taken for public use, without just compensation*: Without the power of eminent domain, which allows the government to purchase property for *public use,* our interstate highways would resemble meandering cow trails. But how to define "public use"? A school or an airport will count, but what about a private development that includes affordable housing? A mall, which the public certainly uses? *Just compensation* is more easily defined: market value, or what any buyer other than the government would pay.

## AMENDMENT VI (RATIFIED IN 1791)

**In all criminal prosecutions, the accused shall enjoy the right to a speedy and public trial, by an impartial jury of the State and district wherein the crime shall have been committed, which district shall have been previously ascertained by law, and to be informed of the nature and cause of the accusation; to be confronted with the witnesses against him; to have compulsory process for obtaining witnesses in his favor, and to have the Assistance of Counsel for his defence.**

The right to a jury trial in criminal cases is proclaimed in Article III, Section 2, Clause 3, but the Sixth Amendment stipulates procedures necessary for a *fair* trial. James Madison and the First Federal Congress, when composing this measure, leaned on a long tradition. Here is how the 1683 Fundamental Constitutions for the Province of East New Jersey, more than a century earlier, provided for *a speedy and public trial* by an *impartial jury of the State and district wherein the crime shall have been committed:*

"No Person or Persons within the said Province shall be . . . condemn'd or Judgment pass'd upon them, but by lawful Judgment of their Peers; neither shall Justice or Right be bought or sold, defered or delayed, to any Person whatsoever: In order to which by the Laws of the Land, all Tryals shall be by twelve Men, and as near as it may be, Peers and Equals, and of the Neighborhood . . . The Manner of returning Juries shall be thus, the Names of all Freeman above five and Twenty Years of Age, within the District of Boroughs out of which the Jury is to be returned, shall be written on equal Pieces of Parchment and put into a Box, and then the Number of the Jury shall be drawn out by a Child under Ten Years of Age."

Most Sixth Amendment provisions are straightforward and can be readily implemented, but if a crime is notorious, it might prove difficult to find an impartial jury in the *district wherein the crime shall have been committed.* Due to local media saturation, some trials have been moved afar, and today's broadcast, electronic, and social media compound the problem. Geographic proximity in 1791 counted for a great deal more than it does today.

## AMENDMENT VII (RATIFIED IN 1791)

**In Suits at common law, where the value in controversy shall exceed twenty dollars, the right of trial by jury shall be preserved, and no fact tried by a jury, shall be otherwise re-examined in any Court of the United States, than according to the rules of the common law.**

*In Suits at common law . . . the right of trial by jury shall be preserved*: Article III, Section 2, Clause 3 guarantees the right to trial in criminal cases; this extends that right to civil cases.

*twenty dollars*: The intent is obvious: juries should not be burdened with petty matters. But why did the First Federal Congress settle on that precise figure? *Twenty dollars* was tacked on at the very last minute by the Senate after the House had passed the amendment without specifying a lower limit. There is no recorded discussion about whether that was too high, too low, or whether there should be a precise limit at all.

It's nice to be clear, but perhaps the Constitution is *too* specific in this case. Despite our overloaded court system and the changing value of money (according to DaveManuel.com's inflation calculator, $20 then would be worth $512.82 today), *twenty dollars* flat stands as the legal threshold today, binding us more than we'd prefer. Do we really need a jury trial to settle a $21 dispute? Why didn't Congress use a more flexible term that could adjust with the times, as it had elsewhere—*unreasonable searches* in the Fourth Amendment, *infamous crime* and *just compensation* in the Fifth, *speedy . . . trial* in the Sixth, and *excessive bail* and *cruel and unusual punishment* in the Eighth? Here, $20 signifies "just too small to bother with," but that cumbersome phrase would never do for our nation's Constitution.

*no fact tried by a jury, shall be otherwise re-examined in any Court of the United States*: Judges are not supposed to overrule juries in matters of fact, but *according to the rules of the common law,* as interpreted by the Supreme Court, a judge can order a new trial to reevaluate the facts.

## AMENDMENT VIII (RATIFIED IN 1791)

**Excessive bail shall not be required, nor excessive fines imposed, nor cruel and unusual punishment inflicted.**

*Excessive bail*: Unlike the Seventh Amendment's *twenty dollars,* this one provides no exact limits for bails and fines. Circumstances will differ, so we must decide what is *excessive* on our own.

*cruel and unusual punishment*: This presents a problem for those who say we must view the Constitution exactly as the framers did. When the Eighth Amendment was written and ratified, public lashing and branding of hands were common punishments for minor offenses. The *cruel and unusual* standard at that time would not have prohibited such practices, yet today, faced with a prisoner's complaint that he was whipped and branded for shoplifting, no judge would deem those punishments constitutional. *Unusual,* by definition, changes with the times, as does our conception of *cruel.*

While branding of hands is no longer current, in some states the death penalty is. Does that constitute *cruel and unusual punishment?* Opinions vary. The First Federal Congress gave us the words, but as with *excessive bail,* it is our business to apply them.

## AMENDMENT IX (RATIFIED IN 1791)

**The enumeration in the Constitution, of certain rights, shall not be construed to deny or disparage others retained by the people.**

During the ratification debates, when critics of the proposed Constitution called for a Bill of Rights, defenders of the new plan argued, disingenuously, that any enumeration of rights would actually be *dangerous.* The very existence of a list, they said, would imply that rights *not* listed were thereby not protected. The Ninth Amendment responds by closing this potential loophole. In practice, however, the Ninth Amendment is of little help in establishing alleged rights not listed. Who is to specify what *others* are *retained by the people*?

During the first third of the twentieth century, the Supreme Court struck down progressive legislation that violated an alleged right to economic liberty or "freedom of contract." Even then, however, it leaned on the due process clauses of the Fifth and Fourteenth Amendments rather than the authority of the Ninth Amendment. After 1937, when the court upheld a state minimum wage law, "freedom of contract" lost its luster.

In *Griswold v. Connecticut* (1965), which struck down a law prohibiting contraception and established precedent cited in *Roe v. Wade* (1973), the Supreme Court ruled that the Constitution protected a "right to privacy," even though that is not specifically listed in the Bill of Rights. Although three justices leaned on the Ninth Amendment, that was not the opinion of the court. The new, unlisted right combined privacy concerns implicit in the First, Third, Fourth, and Fifth Amendments, the court determined, taking some of the load off the Ninth. Justices since then have been reluctant to enunciate a right not listed but *retained by the people* based on the Ninth Amendment alone.

## AMENDMENT X (RATIFIED IN 1791)

**The powers not delegated to the United States by the Constitution, nor prohibited by it to the States, are reserved to the States respectively, or to the people.**

*powers not delegated . . . are reserved to the States*: The Articles of Confederation had declared: "Each state retains . . . every power, jurisdiction, and right, which is not by this confederation expressly delegated to the United States, in Congress assembled." No such provision appears in the body of the Constitution, but during the ratification debates, several state conventions proposed an amendment that would, like the Articles, reserve to the states all powers not "expressly delegated" to the federal government. When James Madison introduced amendments in the First Federal Congress, he included one that closely resembled the state proposals: "The powers not delegated by this constitution, nor prohibited by it to the States, are reserved to the States respectively."

South Carolina representative Thomas Tudor Tucker wondered what happened to the word "expressly." To keep any so-called implied powers from sneaking in, he moved to

reinsert it. Madison opposed the explicit limi-
tation: "It was impossible to confine a Government to the exercise of express powers;
there must necessarily be admitted powers by
implication, unless the Constitution descended
to recount every minutia." Tucker's motion
failed by a vote of 17 to 32. All federal powers
do not need to be "expressly" stipulated, the
First Federal Congress *expressly* decided. For
more than two centuries, states' rights advocates have treated the Tenth Amendment as
if it *did* contain the word "expressly," even
though the amendment's authors (Madison
and the First Federal Congress) made certain it did not. Purposely, the wiggle room
remains.

Historically, the Reserved Powers Amendment has often been cited by opponents of
civil rights legislation, labor laws, and environmental regulations. Since authority in
such matters had not been expressly *delegated* by the Constitution to the federal
government, they argued, it was *reserved to
the States*. In 2010, when the Environmental
Protection Agency cracked down on Texas's
lenient standards for the emission of green-
house gases, Texas conservatives, pointing to
the Tenth Amendment, decried federal over-
reach. But in 2017, when the EPA under

the Trump administration threatened to ban California from imposing emissions requirements that were *stricter* than federal ones, California liberals quickly embraced the Tenth Amendment. By one count, the seven cities in the nation with the worst air pollution were in California. A state's authority to legislate for the safety of its own citizens is surely covered by the Reserved Powers Amendment, they claimed. In both cases, policy disputes over emission standards were cast in constitutional terms—not an uncommon occurrence.

*or to the people*: Following the defeat of "expressly," Roger Sherman moved to add *or to the people* at the end. Although only an afterthought, his motion passed without debate. The body of the Constitution opens with "We the People," and in the Bill of Rights, "the people" literally have the final word.

# Part Three

# LATER AMENDMENTS

## AMENDMENT XI (RATIFIED IN 1795)

**The Judicial power of the United States shall not be construed to extend to any suit in law or equity, commenced or prosecuted against one of the United States by Citizens of another State, or by Citizens or Subjects of any Foreign State.**

According to Article III, Section 2, Clause 1, the *judicial Power* of the federal government extended to *Controversies . . . between a State and Citizens of another State.* State governments at the time complained that this undermined their "sovereign immunity," which insulates sovereign governments from suits by private parties. After the Supreme Court upheld a private suit against Georgia in 1793 (*Chisholm v. Georgia*), states banded together to overturn the *Chisholm v. Georgia* ruling with this constitutional amendment, which prohibits such suits in federal court.

To this day, the Supreme Court struggles with "sovereign immunity." In *Alden v. Maine* (1999), a divided court held that "sovereign immunity derives not from the Eleventh Amendment but from the structure of the original Constitution itself." In response, four dissenting justices complained that the majority was conjuring "a conception of state sovereign immunity" that simply does not appear in the Constitution.

### AMENDMENT XII (RATIFIED IN 1804)

The Electors shall meet in their respective states, and vote by ballot for President and Vice-President, one of whom, at least, shall not be an inhabitant of the same state with themselves; they shall name in their ballots the person voted for as President, and in distinct ballots the person voted for as Vice-President, and they shall make distinct lists of all persons voted for as President, and of all persons voted for as Vice-President, and of the number of votes for each, which lists they shall sign and certify, and transmit sealed to the seat

of the government of the United States,
directed to the President of the Senate;—
The President of the Senate shall, in the
presence of the Senate and House of Representatives, open all the certificates and
the votes shall then be counted;—The person having the greatest number of votes for
President, shall be the President, if such
number be a majority of the whole number of Electors appointed; and if no person
have such majority, then from the persons
having the highest numbers not exceeding
three on the list of those voted for as President, the House of Representatives shall
choose immediately, by ballot, the President. But in choosing the President, the
votes shall be taken by states, the representation from each state having one vote; a
quorum for this purpose shall consist of
a member or members from two-thirds of
the states, and a majority of all the states
shall be necessary to a choice. ~~And if the
House of Representatives shall not choose
a President whenever the right of choice
shall devolve upon them, before the fourth
day of March next following, then the Vice-
President shall act as President, as in the
case of the death or other constitutional
disability of the President.~~ The person hav-

ing the greatest number of votes as Vice-President, shall be the Vice-President, if such number be a majority of the whole number of Electors appointed, and if no person have a majority, then from the two highest numbers on the list, the Senate shall choose the Vice-President; a quorum for the purpose shall consist of two-thirds of the whole number of Senators, and a majority of the whole number shall be necessary to a choice. But no person constitutionally ineligible to the office of President shall be eligible to that of Vice-President of the United States.

The key phrase in this lengthy text is *distinct ballots.* Under the original Constitution, presidential electors cast two ballots but did not specify which was for president and which for vice president. That system was easily gamed, with disastrous consequences.

On January 25, 1789, ten days before electors were to assemble in their respective state capitals to vote for the first president and vice president under the new Constitution, Alexander Hamilton made a remarkable admission: "Every body is aware of that defect in the constitution which renders it possible that the man intended for Vice President may in fact turn up President." The "defect" was that each elector voted for two candidates without distinguishing between president and vice president.

In 1800, Hamilton's fear was almost realized. By then Americans had split into two parties, Federalists and Republicans. Since neither party could get its way without controlling the presidency, each decided to rally behind a candidate of its choosing. Caucusing in Philadelphia, Federalist leaders decided to back the sitting president, John Adams, while Republican leaders opted for the sitting vice president, Thomas Jefferson, who had come in second in the balloting for president in 1796. This time Jefferson received seventy-three electoral votes and Adams sixty-five, but that did not make Jefferson president. Aaron Burr also received seventy-three electoral votes because every single Republican elector, true to party unity, voted for both Jefferson and Burr.

That sent the election into the House of Representatives, with each state delegation receiving one vote. The Constitution stipulated that a *Majority of all the States shall be necessary* to determine the winner, but there were sixteen states at the time, and Republicans constituted a majority in only eight delegations—one shy of a majority. So for Jefferson to become president, he would need the support of at least one state delegation that was not Republican.

Federalists saw an opportunity to deny Jefferson the presidency by casting all their votes for Aaron Burr. If they could convince just a few Republican congressmen to go with Burr, he would become president—and even though he was a Republican, he would owe the Federalists for placing him there.

The House took votes again and again—thirty-three times over a four-day period—but no winner emerged. Republican governors of the two largest states, Virginia and Pennsylvania, threatened to mobilize their militias. Federalists countered by boasting that the well-drilled militias of New England could trounce them. Finally, a handful of Federalists from key states decided that obstructionist tactics must end before a civil war broke out. On the thirty-sixth ballot, the House of Representatives determined that Thomas Jefferson would be the next president.

Following this fiasco, both parties agreed that the system needed fixing. The Twelfth Amendment, ratified in 1804, established separate ballots for president and vice president. That eliminated one glitch, but it did not solve the basic problems of the elector system. The framers had assumed that electors would be chosen for their greater wisdom and exercise discretion, but once two parties emerged, each naturally put forth a set of electors pledged to vote a certain way. That is how it's done to this day.

In a pamphlet penned during the ratification debates, the ardent Federalist Noah Webster had boasted, "The president of the United States is elective, and what is a capital improvement on the best governments, the mode of choosing him excludes the danger of faction and corruption." But in 1800, next to these words in a personal copy of his own pamphlet, he jotted down, "This proves how little dependence can be placed on theory. Twelve years experience, or four elections, demonstrates the contrary."

## AMENDMENT XIII (RATIFIED IN 1865)

### SECTION 1.

Neither slavery nor involuntary servitude, except as a punishment for crime whereof the party shall have been duly convicted, shall exist within the United States, or any place subject to their jurisdiction.

## SECTION 2.

**Congress shall have power to enforce this article by appropriate legislation.**

It took the Civil War to get there, but the United States at last prohibited what Gouverneur Morris, at the Constitutional Convention, called America's "nefarious institution" and "the curse of heaven." Two years earlier, President Lincoln's Emancipation Proclamation had freed only those slaves held in areas that were "in rebellion against the United States"—by definition, places where Lincoln's executive order would not be recognized. The proclamation was transformative because of what it signaled, but it purposely did not end slavery in states within the Union—Lincoln could not afford to alienate border states that had not seceded but still permitted slavery. At the close of the war, however, the Thirteenth Amendment dealt the death knell to legalized slavery throughout the United States.

## AMENDMENT XIV (RATIFIED IN 1868)

### SECTION 1.

**All persons born or naturalized in the United States, and subject to the juris-**

diction thereof, are citizens of the United States and of the State wherein they reside. No State shall make or enforce any law which shall abridge the privileges or immunities of citizens of the United States; nor shall any State deprive any person of life, liberty, or property, without due process of law; nor deny to any person within its jurisdiction the equal protection of the laws.

### SECTION 2.

Representatives shall be apportioned among the several States according to their respective numbers, counting the whole number of persons in each State, excluding Indians not taxed. But when the right to vote at any election for the choice of electors for President and Vice President of the United States, Representatives in Congress, the Executive and Judicial officers of a State, or the members of the Legislature thereof, is denied to any of the male inhabitants of such State, being twenty-one years of age, and citizens of the United States, or in any way abridged, except for participation in rebellion, or other crime, the basis of representation therein shall be reduced in the proportion which the number of such male citizens shall bear to the whole number of male citizens twenty-one years of age in such State.

### SECTION 3.

No person shall be a Senator or Representative in Congress, or elector of President and Vice President, or hold any office, civil or military, under the United States, or under any State, who, having previously taken an oath, as a member of Congress, or as an officer of the United States, or as a member of any State legislature, or as an executive or judicial officer of any State, to support the Constitution of the United States, shall have engaged in insurrection or rebellion against the same, or given aid or comfort to the enemies thereof. But Congress may, by a vote of two-thirds of each House, remove such disability.

### SECTION 4.

The validity of the public debt of the United States, authorized by law, including debts incurred for payment of pensions and bounties for services in suppressing insurrection or rebellion, shall not be questioned. But neither the United States nor any State shall assume or pay any debt or obligation incurred in aid of insurrection or rebellion against the United States, or any claim for the loss or emancipation of any slave; but all such debts, obligations and claims shall be held illegal and void.

## SECTION 5.

The Congress shall have power to enforce, by appropriate legislation, the provisions of this article.

The Thirteenth Amendment was a promising start but clearly not enough. Although Southern state legislatures, under duress, agreed to ratify it, they simultaneously declared that it did not grant the federal government authority to determine the "political status" of former slaves. That would be left to the states, they maintained. Radical Republicans, who controlled Congress, responded by proposing the Fourteenth Amendment, and they would not allow the rebellious states to rejoin the Union until they voted to ratify it.

The Fourteenth Amendment transformed the Constitution, shifting the balance of authority away from the states and toward the federal government. The South had taken "states' rights" to the furthest reach: secession. Henceforth, the federal government would limit the authority of a state to define, and thereby govern, its own citizenry. Under federal watch, citizenry became more inclusive, while the rights of citizens expanded.

Section 1, the heart of the amendment, is the most sweeping clause in the Constitution and, not coincidentally, among the most litigated.

*All persons born or naturalized in the United States . . . are citizens of the United States*: In *Dred Scott v. Sanford* (1857), the Supreme Court declared that people of African ancestry, who had been carried to America as slaves, could never be citizens of the United States. The Fourteenth Amendment opens with a clear refutation of that decision. Today, in a very different context, this provision has proved controversial: Should children of illegal immigrants really be granted automatic citizenship? Back then, this was a nonissue; there were no illegal immigrants because the nation had yet to pass laws excluding immigrants.

*No State shall . . . abridge the privileges or immunities of citizens of the United States*: This wording echoes Article IV, Section 2, Clause 1. There, citizens of one state are guaranteed the *privileges* and *immunities* of all other states; here, states are prohibited from interfering with guarantees inherent in federal citizenship.

*nor shall any State deprive any person of life, liberty, or property, without due process of law*: This wording echoes the due process provision in the Fifth Amendment. Previously, the Supreme Court had not protected rights listed in the first ten amendments from incursions by state governments; only Congress was prohibited from violating those rights. Under the Fourteenth Amendment, states, too, were obligated to protect *life, liberty, or property* by applying *due process of law.* In this way, the Fourteenth Amendment broadened the scope of most rights enumerated in the Bill of Rights—the doctrine of "incorporation" mentioned in the discussion of the First Amendment. Only after the Fourteenth Amendment and incorporation did the Bill of Rights figure prominently in American culture and American jurisprudence.

*nor deny to any person within its jurisdiction the equal protection of the laws*: In the context of the times, *any person* was shorthand for a former slave who was being denied equal protection of the laws in Southern states. Subsequently, however, it has come to mean exactly what it says: *any per-*

*son.* A legal foundation for America's celebrated diversity, the *equal protection* clause
of the Fourteenth Amendment buttresses a
plethora of civil rights legislation that now
protects the rights of women, religious and
ethnic minorities, disabled people, the LGBT
community, and . . .

And corporations! In the first half of the
nineteenth century, the Supreme Court
held that corporations were contracts that
enjoyed protection of the laws, including
the same rights of ownership that people
had. With that precedent set, the Fourteenth
Amendment's guarantee of *equal protection
of the laws* was red meat for corporate lawyers. In *Santa Clara County v. Southern Pacific Railroad Company* (1886), the Supreme
Court assumed that corporations, like former slaves, were entitled to equal protection,
and two years later, in *Pembina Consolidated
Silver Mining Co. v. Pennsylvania,* the court
stated outright: "A private corporation is
included under the designation of person in
the Fourteenth Amendment to the Constitution, Section I." And so it would be. Supreme
Court justices who adhere to the doctrine
of original intent or original meaning should
shudder at the idea that the Reconstruction

Congress intended to protect corporations—but justices allow that to slide, choosing not to disrupt the large body of law based on "corporate personhood."

Section 2. *Representatives shall be apportioned . . . counting the whole number of persons in each State*: Whole persons, not three-fifths as stipulated in the original Constitution—but only if those now-whole persons have *the right to vote*. Southern states cannot have it both ways, as they did when they got extra votes for slaves who could not vote.

Section 3. Former rebels who had held state or federal office before the Civil War could not return to positions of power, unless permitted by supermajorities in the House and Senate.

Section 4. The United States would make good on its war debt but not on the debt of those who rebelled against it, nor would it pay former masters for the people they once held in bondage.

Section 5. Congress has the authority to enforce the Fourteenth Amendment. Enforcement clauses are included in several amendments, but this one packed an extra punch. The Reconstruction Congress passed

sweeping legislation that might appear dicta-
torial, but it could justify those laws by pointing to Section 5.

## AMENDMENT XV (RATIFIED IN 1870)

### SECTION 1.

**The right of citizens of the United States
to vote shall not be denied or abridged by
the United States or by any State on account
of race, color, or previous condition of
servitude.**

### SECTION 2.

**The Congress shall have power to enforce
this article by appropriate legislation.**

This was the last of three Reconstruction Era
amendments pushed by Radical Republicans
in Congress. When we speak of the Constitution's "framers," we need to include
the Reconstruction Congress as well as the
First Federal Congress, which drafted the Bill
of Rights. The Thirteenth Amendment abol-
ished slavery, the Fourteenth Amendment
extended citizenship to include former slaves,
and the Fifteenth Amendment granted them

the right to exercise the defining *act* of citizenship: voting.

But the right of African Americans to vote, it turned out, was not a done deal. During Reconstruction, under federal scrutiny, former slaves in the South did vote, and many were even elected to governmental offices—but once the federal presence disappeared, with it went implementation of the Fifteenth Amendment. Southern states instituted poll taxes (which poor blacks couldn't pay) and biased literacy tests ("See Dick and Jane run" for whites, obscure provisions in state constitutions for blacks). Further, "grandfather clauses" exempted citizens from the literacy requirement if their grandfathers had been eligible to vote. This enabled poor whites to keep the franchise while implicitly excluding all blacks. (Few former slaves were *legal* descendants of a grandfather who could vote, although many, off the books, had white grandfathers.) Not until the mid-twentieth century were these Jim Crow obstructions to the Fifteenth Amendment curtailed through acts of Congress, executive orders, and, for the poll tax, by the Twenty-Fourth Amendment.

## AMENDMENT XVI (RATIFIED IN 1913)

**The Congress shall have power to lay and collect taxes on incomes, from whatever source derived, without apportionment among the several States, and without regard to any census or enumeration.**

This is often misnamed "the income tax amendment." Not so. Congress had financed the Civil War in large measure by a graduated income tax: 3 percent for incomes between $600 and $10,000 and 5 percent tax on incomes in excess of $10,000. The Supreme Court at that time treated income taxes as indirect taxes, authorized by Article I, Section 8, Clause 1 of the Constitution.

But in *Pollock v. Farmers' Loan and Trust Company* (1895), the court overturned precedent and declared that taxing income derived from rents, interest, and dividends functioned as a *direct* tax; therefore, under Article I, Section 9, Clause 4, such a tax had to be proportioned according to the state populations. That would mean that people in a poor state, to produce that state's share, would be taxed at a *higher* rate than people in a rich state.

Strangely, the *Pollock* ruling stated that

income from *labor* was an indirect tax and therefore did *not* have to be proportioned. This meant that Congress could tax working people freely. On the other hand, taxing rent, interest, and dividends—how wealthy people make money—would have to be done in a ridiculously unfair manner, with the poor paying higher rates than the rich. Workers cried foul. They pushed for, and got, an amendment that lifted the *apportionment* requirement from *all* income taxes. Read the wording again, and you will get the point. The original Constitution had not prohibited income taxes, and the Sixteenth Amendment made them workable.

### AMENDMENT XVII (RATIFIED IN 1913)

The Senate of the United States shall be composed of two Senators from each State, elected by the people thereof, for six years; and each Senator shall have one vote. The electors in each State shall have the qualifications requisite for electors of the most numerous branch of the State legislatures.

When vacancies happen in the representation of any State in the Senate, the executive authority of such State shall issue writs of election to fill such vacancies: Provided, That the legislature of any State may empower the executive thereof to make temporary appointments until the people fill the vacancies by election as the legislature may direct.

This amendment shall not be so construed as to affect the election or term of any Senator chosen before it becomes valid as part of the Constitution.

Like the Sixteenth Amendment, ratified the same year, the Seventeenth was propelled by popular outcry. Article I, Section 3, Clause 1 stipulated that senators be chosen by state legislatures, but in the Gilded Age money talked, and money could induce a state legislature to select a particular senator. The push for direct election of senators started in the 1890s, but a constitutional amendment had to overcome two major hurdles: (1) It had to gain approval from two-thirds of the United States senators, all of whom owed their positions to state legislatures. (2) It had to be ratified by three-quarters of the state legislatures, bodies that stood to lose significant power by no longer selecting senators. Against such

odds, its subsequent passage speaks greatly
to the power of the people.

## AMENDMENT XVIII (RATIFIED IN 1919)

### SECTION 1.

~~After one year from the ratification of this
article the manufacture, sale, or transportation of intoxicating liquors within, the
importation thereof into, or the exporta-
tion thereof from the United States and
all the territory subject to the jurisdiction
thereof for beverage purposes is hereby
prohibited.~~

### SECTION 2.

~~The Congress and the several States shall
have concurrent power to enforce this article by appropriate legislation.~~

### SECTION 3.

~~This article shall be inoperative unless it
shall have been ratified as an amendment
to the Constitution by the legislatures of
the several States, as provided in the Constitution, within seven years from the date
of the submission hereof to the States by
the Congress.~~

Prohibition! We are all familiar with this amendment and its effect on American life and culture, but how many have pondered the constitutional aspects of prohibition? The Eighteenth Amendment was an outlier. No other clause or amendment gives Congress and the states *concurrent* powers of enforcement. Booze was deemed so bad that all governmental forces were enlisted to fight it.

Prohibition was pushed by multiple advocacy groups: wives tired of their husbands frittering away paychecks at taverns and coming home drunk and violent, religious moralists, nativists profiling immigrants deemed to be boozers, and country folk punishing cities and their evil ways. But this experiment in constitutional lawmaking did not turn out well. Stay tuned for the Twenty-First Amendment.

### AMENDMENT XIX (RATIFIED IN 1920)

**The right of citizens of the United States to vote shall not be denied or abridged by the United States or by any State on account of sex.**

**Congress shall have power to enforce this article by appropriate legislation.**

Note the identical wording to Section 1 of the Fifteenth Amendment, with *sex* taking the place of *race, color, or previous condition of servitude.* Why had the Fifteenth Amendment, which guaranteed blacks the right to vote, not included women, who had to wait another half a century?

After the Civil War, granting African Americans the right to vote was controversial enough, in the North as well as in the South. Some suffragettes, recognizing that combining the two issues might doom them both, were willing to "wait their turn," as male reformers requested them to do. Others were sorely disappointed that women were not included and tried to push the matter in court; they claimed, unsuccessfully, that women were being denied *equal protection of the laws,* which Section 1 of the Fourteenth Amendment demanded.

The split in the suffrage movement continued for a generation. Unable to amass a unified national campaign, activists turned to the states—and that is where their battle was ultimately won. Before the Constitution guaranteed women throughout the nation the right to vote, fifteen states granted suffrage for all elections; eight more allowed women to vote in presidential elections; and in most other states, women could vote in primaries or local elections. Only seven states kept women from the ballot box in all elections.

As momentum mounted, there was one last hurdle, resistance from antitemperance interests: brewers, distillers, and drinkers. The temperance movement was dominated by women, and everybody knew that once women got the franchise, prohibition would surely follow. In fact, that played out in reverse. Note the ratification dates for the Eighteenth Amendment (1919) and the Nineteenth Amendment (1920). Once prohibition had been written into the Constitution, one prime reason to *deny* women the vote disappeared.

## AMENDMENT XX (RATIFIED IN 1933)

### SECTION 1.

The terms of the President and Vice President shall end at noon on the 20th day of January, and the terms of Senators and Representatives at noon on the 3d day of January, of the years in which such terms would have ended if this article had not been ratified; and the terms of their successors shall then begin.

## SECTION 2.

The Congress shall assemble at least once in every year, and such meeting shall begin at noon on the 3d day of January, unless they shall by law appoint a different day.

## SECTION 3.

If, at the time fixed for the beginning of the term of the President, the President elect shall have died, the Vice President elect shall become President. If a President shall not have been chosen before the time fixed for the beginning of his term, or if the President elect shall have failed to qualify, then the Vice President elect shall act as President until a President shall have qualified; and the Congress may by law provide for the case wherein neither a President elect nor a Vice President elect shall have qualified, declaring who shall then act as President, or the manner in which one who is to act shall be selected, and such person shall act accordingly until a President or Vice President shall have qualified.

## SECTION 4.

The Congress may by law provide for the case of the death of any of the persons from whom the House of Representatives may choose a President whenever the right of choice shall have devolved upon them, and for the case of the death of any of the persons from whom the Senate may choose a Vice President whenever the right of choice shall have devolved upon them.

### SECTION 5.

Sections 1 and 2 shall take effect on the 15th day of October following the ratification of this article.

### SECTION 6.

This article shall be inoperative unless it shall have been ratified as an amendment to the Constitution by the legislatures of three-fourths of the several States within seven years from the date of its submission.

These are housekeeping measures. Sections 1 and 2 bring the government's calendar up to date, lessening the duration of "lame duck" presidencies and sessions of Congress. Previously, the president and members of Congress would not take office until March 4 of the year following their elections.

Sections 3 and 4 refine the procedures for

succession of the president, which would be specified in even greater detail by the Twenty-Fifth Amendment.

Sections 5 and 6 determine how and when the amendment is to take effect.

## AMENDMENT XXI (RATIFIED IN 1933)

### SECTION 1.

The eighteenth article of amendment to the Constitution of the United States is hereby repealed.

### SECTION 2.

The transportation or importation into any State, Territory, or possession of the United States for delivery or use therein of intoxicating liquors, in violation of the laws thereof, is hereby prohibited.

### SECTION 3.

This article shall be inoperative unless it shall have been ratified as an amendment to the Constitution by conventions in the several States, as provided in the Constitution, within seven years from the date of the submission hereof to the States by the Congress.

The Twenty-First Amendment is known for the final word in Section 1, *repealed*. Prohibition is over, so let the drinking begin! But wait: What about Section 2? Read it carefully, and note the final two words there: *hereby prohibited*. Was "prohibition" really over?

Now compare Section 2 of the Twenty-First Amendment with Section 2 of the Eighteenth Amendment. There, Congress and the states had *concurrent* power to prohibit intoxicating beverages; here, the authority to outlaw the possession or delivery of liquor is granted exclusively to the states. Despite the repeal of national prohibition, Mississippi, North Carolina, Kansas, Oklahoma, and Texas remained dry. Most other states established minimum drinking ages.

Constitution wonks might notice a potential conflict between Article I, Section 8, Clause 3, which gives Congress the authority to *regulate commerce . . . among the several states,* and the stipulation here that a state has the authority to regulate the importation of liquor into its jurisdiction. The Supreme Court has noted that, too. In *Granholm v. Heald* (2005), the issue came to a head. Michigan's Liquor Control Code prohibited the direct delivery of out-of-state wines to Michigan consumers, basing its authority on

Section 2 of the Twenty-First Amendment. (Although their motive was to favor in-state wineries, state officials claimed the measure would help prevent sale to minors.) Twelve wine connoisseurs objected to the state's interference with interstate commerce. In a 5–4 decision, the court decided that the interstate commerce clause trumped the Twenty-First Amendment. (FYI, Constitution wonks: Antonin Scalia and Ruth Ginsburg sided with the majority, while John Paul Stevens and Clarence Thomas dissented—strange alliances indeed.)

## AMENDMENT XXII (RATIFIED IN 1951)

### SECTION 1.

No person shall be elected to the office of the President more than twice, and no person who has held the office of President, or acted as President, for more than two years of a term to which some other person was elected President shall be elected to the office of the President more than once. But this article shall not apply to any person holding the office of President when this article was proposed by the Congress, and shall not prevent any person who may be holding the office of President, or acting as President, during the term within which this article becomes operative from holding the office of President or acting as President during the remainder of such term.

### SECTION 2.

This article shall be inoperative unless it shall have been ratified as an amendment to the Constitution by the legislatures of three-fourths of the several states within seven years from the date of its submission to the states by the Congress.

George Washington served the nation in many ways, including knowing when to retire. At the close of the Revolutionary War, he and the army he commanded could have seized the reins of a nearly dysfunctional government, but he returned to private life instead. In 1796, after two terms as president, he declined to seek a third. That set a precedent that other presidents, however popular, would follow—until Franklin Delano Roosevelt sought and received a third term in 1940 and a fourth in 1944. Admittedly, with the Depression and World War II, those were trying times, but even so, Americans of both parties worried of the precedent that set.

The framers had rejected "rotation in office" (what we call term limits) for the presidency. The Twenty-Second Amendment requires it.

## AMENDMENT XXIII (RATIFIED IN 1961)

### SECTION 1.

The District constituting the seat of Government of the United States shall appoint in such manner as the Congress may direct:

A number of electors of President and Vice President equal to the whole number of Senators and Representatives in Congress to which the District would be entitled if it were a State, but in no event more than the least populous State; they shall be in addition to those appointed by the States, but they shall be considered, for the purposes of the election of President and Vice President, to be electors appointed by a State; and they shall meet in the District and perform such duties as provided by the twelfth article of amendment.

### SECTION 2.

The Congress shall have power to enforce this article by appropriate legislation.

The District of Columbia is a unique crea-
tion, established pursuant to Article I, Section 8, Clause 17 of the Constitution. To
ensure that residents of the nation's capital
would not have undue influence over the
federal government, the framers gave them
*no* influence, at least on paper. They might
lobby, but at least they could not vote. That
made sense when the nation's capital was a
place where people worked, not lived—but
by 1960, Washington, D. C., had become the
ninth-largest city in the nation, and depriving
people who live there of the franchise did not
seem just. Hence the Twenty-Third Amendment, which, in substance, allows residents
of the nation's capital to vote for president.
(Note the excess verbiage, however. Technically, neither citizens of the District of Columbia nor anybody else can vote directly for the
president; we only choose electors, unknown
to us personally but pledged to the candidate
of our choice.)

Why the franchise for president but not for
Congress? Unlike residents of states, people
who live in Washington, D. C., are still sub-
jected to "taxation without representation"—a
major complaint that led to American independence. In 1978, Congress proposed an
amendment that would grant full voting rights

for Washington, D. C., "as though it were a state." That seems fair enough, but residents there are overwhelmingly Democrats, and Republicans did not wish to give the opposing party two more seats in the Senate and at least one more seat in the House. Only sixteen states voted to ratify the District of Columbia Voting Rights Amendment, less than half of the thirty-eight required. Today, with partisanship at a fever pitch, this amendment would probably not clear the first hurdle, two-thirds majorities in both houses of Congress.

## AMENDMENT XXIV (RATIFIED IN 1964)

### SECTION 1.

The right of citizens of the United States to vote in any primary or other election for President or Vice President, for electors for President or Vice President, or for Senator or Representative in Congress, shall not be denied or abridged by the United States or any State by reason of failure to pay any poll tax or other tax.

### SECTION 2.

The Congress shall have power to enforce this article by appropriate legislation.

Prohibiting the *poll tax* on citizens wishing to vote—what Article I, Section 9, Clause 3 calls a *Capitation* tax—eliminated a common ploy used by Southern states to keep African Americans from voting. Although the Twenty-Fourth Amendment covers only federal elections, the Supreme Court, in *Harper v. Virginia Board of Elections* (1966), used the Fourteenth Amendment's *equal protection* guarantee to prohibit poll taxes for state elections as well.

In the Voting Rights Act of 1965, Congress clamped down on literacy tests, grandfather clauses, and other techniques that skirted the Fifteenth Amendment. It also established a means for determining which districts were practicing discriminatory actions, and it required those offenders to seek preapproval from the Attorney General before instituting any new franchise regulations. For half a century, this enabled the federal government to prevent backsliding by recalcitrant states, but in *Shelby County v. Holder* (2013), the Supreme Court struck down the formula for determining discrimination, effectively ending the need for preapproval. That is the historical and constitutional background for today's heated debate: Are the plethora of new voting regulations at the state level reasonable protections against alleged "voter fraud"? Or are they designed to inhibit voting by targeted groups, thereby violating the letter of the Fourteenth Amendment (equal protection) and the spirit of the Fifteenth Amendment? The consequences here are profound, both politically and philosophically.

## AMENDMENT XXV (RATIFIED IN 1967)

### SECTION 1.

In case of the removal of the President from office or of his death or resignation, the Vice President shall become President.

### SECTION 2.

Whenever there is a vacancy in the office of the Vice President, the President shall nominate a Vice President who shall take office upon confirmation by a majority vote of both Houses of Congress.

### SECTION 3.

Whenever the President transmits to the President pro tempore of the Senate and the Speaker of the House of Representatives his written declaration that he is unable to discharge the powers and duties of his office, and until he transmits to them a written declaration to the contrary, such powers and duties shall be discharged by the Vice President as Acting President.

### SECTION 4.

Whenever the Vice President and a majority of either the principal officers of the executive departments or of such other body as Congress may by law provide, transmit to the President pro tempore of the Senate and the Speaker of the House of Representatives their written declaration that the President is unable to discharge the powers and duties of his office, the Vice President shall immediately assume the powers and duties of the office as Acting President.

Thereafter, when the President transmits to the President pro tempore of the Senate and the Speaker of the House of Representatives his written declaration that no inability exists, he shall resume the powers and duties of his office unless the Vice President and a majority of either the principal officers of the executive department or of such other body as Congress may by law provide, transmit within four days to the

President pro tempore of the Senate and the Speaker of the House of Representatives their written declaration that the President is unable to discharge the powers and duties of his office. Thereupon Congress shall decide the issue, assembling within forty-eight hours for that purpose if not in session. If the Congress, within twenty-one days after receipt of the latter written declaration, or, if Congress is not in session, within twenty-one days after Congress is required to assemble, determines by two-thirds vote of both Houses that the President is unable to discharge the powers and duties of his office, the Vice President shall continue to discharge the same as Acting President; otherwise, the President shall resume the powers and duties of his office.

The Twenty-Fifth Amendment resolves an ambiguity in Article II, Section 1, Clause 6 of the Constitution: When assuming *the powers and duties* of the presidency, does a vice president do so as an *acting* president or as an *actual* president, one entitled to remain in office for the remainder of the four-year term? (Historically, vice presidents had become actual presidents upon the death of their predecessors, but that was nowhere stated in the Constitution.) Section 1 states that the vice president becomes an actual president if the sitting president either dies or resigns, while Section 3 stipulates that if a president declares to Congress *that he is unable to discharge the powers and duties* of the office, the vice president serves only as an *Acting President*. Before President Ronald Reagan underwent elective surgery in 1985, he officially passed the office to Vice President George H. W. Bush, who served as an acting president for less than eight hours. These provisions are straightforward, as is Section 2, which stipulates how a new vice president is to be selected if the office becomes open.

Section 4 is more complicated. What happens if a president is unfit to serve yet cannot declare that? In 1881, President James A. Garfield, shot by an assassin, was in and out of a coma for seventy-nine days before dying; during that time, Vice President Chester A. Arthur did not command the office of the president. If a similar event happened now, the vice president, with support from either the cabinet or some other body of Congress's choosing, could become the *Acting President* until the president either dies or becomes able to resume the duties of the office.

Imagine, however, that a president becomes incapacitated but does not realize it or refuses to acknowledge it. In 1987, during President Reagan's second term, he ceased reading briefs and spent much of his time watching movies, which concerned some of his aides. Chief of Staff Howard Baker set up a test situation, a luncheon, where he and other Reagan associates were to scrutinize the president's behavior for signs of incompetence. Reagan performed well and was deemed fit for office. What if he had not passed this test? Vice President Bush could have convened the cabinet, submitted a declaration to Congress, and immediately assumed the duties of the presidency, although only as an *Acting President*—but if Reagan believed he *was* fully capable, he could simply declare as much and resume his duties. At this point, to dislodge the president, the burden of proof would be on the vice president and either the cabinet or another body designated by Congress. In such a "contested removal," as it is called, the final arbiter is Congress and the bar is high: a two-thirds supermajority, as with an impeachment trial.

The framers hadn't accounted for an incapacitated president. Had they done so, they probably would not have granted the vice president a lead role in a procedure that could elevate him to the presidency. But those who drafted the Twenty-Fifth Amendment did not want the process to be politicized and determined that any move to dislodge a president for incapacity had to emerge from within his own party.

This amendment was already under discussion when John F. Kennedy was assassinated in 1963. That tragic event provided a sense of urgency: What would have happened if Kennedy had survived but lay in a coma like President Garfield? Ratification was swift and almost unanimous: forty-seven states in less than two years.

## AMENDMENT XXVI (RATIFIED IN 1971)

### SECTION 1.

The right of citizens of the United States, who are eighteen years of age or older, to vote shall not be denied or abridged by the United States or by any State on account of age.

### SECTION 2.

The Congress shall have the power to enforce this article by appropriate legislation.

"Old enough to fight, old enough to vote."
With hundreds of thousands of soldiers
under the age of twenty-one serving in Vietnam, many involuntarily, this amendment
was difficult to oppose. In 1970, by amending the 1965 Voting Rights Act, Congress
lowered the voting age to 18, but in *Oregon
v. Mitchell* (1970), a sharply divided Supreme
Court ruled that Congress could only do so
for federal elections. Congress's reaction was
immediate. By unanimous vote of the Senate, and 401–19 in the House, it proposed
the Twenty-Sixth Amendment. The speed of
ratification by the states broke all records:
three months and one week.

## AMENDMENT XXVII (RATIFIED IN 1992)

**No law, varying the compensation for the
services of the Senators and Representatives, shall take effect, until an election of
Representatives shall have intervened.**

If the Twenty-Sixth Amendment was the
quickest, the Twenty-Seventh was far and
away the slowest. It was initially proposed by
the First Federal Congress in 1789, along with
ten amendments that would become the Bill

of Rights—and on Congress's list, it actually preceded what is now the First Amendment. We do not know why some states turned it down back then, but in any case, it failed to clear the three-quarters threshold. For almost two hundred years the amendment lay nearly dormant—and then came an only-in-America story of a lifetime.

In March 1982, University of Texas student Gregory Watson, while researching a term paper, came upon this unratified amendment. Prohibiting members of Congress from giving themselves pay raises was an idea whose time had come, he thought. Article V of the Constitution did not specify a time frame for ratification of amendments, and by then nine had already assented. Couldn't other states now jump onboard?

Watson's paper received a C, but he pushed on. Congress's unpopularity certainly helped, and besides, the amendment made sense. Congress could still raise its pay, but before any individual member could take advantage of that, the voters would get a chance to weigh in. Politically, it was nearly impossible to oppose, and finally, 203 years later, one of the first amendments Congress proposed became the last (as of this date) to be ratified.

Perhaps we should end with that, but alas, there could be trouble ahead. Is it really a good idea to let an amendment linger that long?

Those who drafted the Eighteenth, Twentieth, Twenty-First, and Twenty-Second Amendments placed a statute of limitations of seven years for ratification, and that, very likely, was how the framers envisioned the amendment process. A three-quarters supermajority for constitutional amendments is the stiffest requirement they imposed for any governmental action, undoubtedly for a reason. But if some states ratify an amendment now, and others the next generation, and yet others generations hence, that amendment, although ratified, might never have had more than lukewarm support at a given time.

Alas, nobody ever said drafting a constitution would be easy, and interpreting the United States Constitution can be yet more difficult. Debates are inevitable, and user discretion is always advised. But as we ponder this section or that, we should never lose sight of the Constitution's overarching purpose: to establish a *workable government* that meets the people's needs. Attempts to subvert the very idea of government in the name of the Constitution are, in spirit, unconstitutional.

## ABOUT THE AUTHOR

Ray Raphael's ten books on the Founding Era include *A People's History of the American Revolution* (2001), *Founding Myths: Stories That Hide Our Patriotic Past* (2004), *Mr. President: How and Why the Founders Created a Chief Executive* (2012), and *Constitutional Myths* (2013). Having taught at Humboldt State University and College of the Redwoods, he is currently developing teaching tools for the Constitutional Sources Project (ConSource) and serving as an associate editor for the *Journal of the American Revolution*. He lives in Northern California.

ALSO BY

# RAY RAPHAEL

MR. PRESIDENT

*How and Why the Founders Created a Chief Executive*

For the first time, by focusing closely on the dynamic give-and-take at the Constitutional Convention, Ray Raphael reveals how politics and personalities cobbled together a lasting but flawed executive office. Charting the presidency as it evolved during the administrations of Washington, Adams, and Jefferson, Raphael shows how, given the Constitution's broad outlines, the president's powers could easily be augmented but rarely diminished. Today we see the result—an office that has become more sweeping, more powerful, and more inherently partisan than the framers ever intended. And the issues of 1787—whether the Electoral College, the president's war powers, or the extent of executive authority—continue to stir our political debates.

History

REVOLUTIONARY FOUNDERS

*Rebels, Radicals, and Reformers in the Making of the Nation*

Edited by Alfred F. Young and Gary Nash

In twenty-two original essays, leading historians reveal the radical impulses at the founding of the American Republic. Here is a fresh, new reading of the American Revolution that gives voice and recognition to a generation of radical thinkers and doers whose revolutionary ideals outstripped those of the "Founding Fathers." While the Founding Fathers advocated a break from Britain and espoused ideals of republican government, none proposed significant changes to the fabric of colonial society. Yet during this "revolutionary" period some people did believe that "liberty" meant "liberty for all" and that "equality" should be applied to political, economic, and religious spheres. Here are the stories of individuals and groups who exemplified the radical ideals of the American Revolution more in keeping with our own values today. This volume helps us to understand the social conflicts unleashed by the struggle for independence, the Revolution's achievements, and the unfinished agenda it left to future generations to confront.

History

VINTAGE BOOKS
Available wherever books are sold.
www.vintagebooks.com